Lords of Dalkeith

Lords of Dalkeith

A history of Dalkeith Palace and its inhabitants

KENNETH SCOTT

First published in hardback by Argyll Publishing, an imprint of Capercaillie Books in 2014.

This paperback edition published by Capercaillie Books, Edinburgh 2016.

Registered Office 1 Rutland Court, Edinburgh

A catalogue record of this book is available from the British Library

ISBN 978-1-909305-87-8

Printed and bound by Bell & Bain Ltd., Glasgow

Design and typeset by 3btype.com

For Anna, Andrew and Angus

On the edge of the town of Dalkeith, seven miles south-east of Edinburgh, lies an extensive country park, part of the old Caledonian Forest. It is watered by two rivers, the North and South Esk, which merge near the northern end of the park and then flow north into the Firth of Forth. The park contains an elegant stable block and coach house of 1748 by William Adam, a splendid bridge over the North Esk designed by his son Robert Adam in 1792, an ornate twelve-sided conservatory of 1832 by William Burn, and, perhaps now its most popular feature, an excellent children's adventure playground, currently being developed with the addition of a Visitor Centre.

Dominating the park, on a high ridge above the North Esk, stands Dalkeith House, perhaps the grandest of all early classical mansions in Scotland and known through out much of its history as Dalkeith Palace. It was built in its present form in the first decade of the eighteenth century by James Smith for Anna, Duchess of Buccleuch, and was until the First World War a ducal seat of great magnificence, filled with fine furniture and works of art. All that has gone, and the house though still owned by the Duke of Buccleuch is now a student residence and study centre for the University of Wisconsin; but the house itself, and the earlier castle and palace which stood on this site, have a long and colourful history dating back to at least the twelfth century.

Sir Kenneth Scott gives an illuminating account of the history of this palace and chronicles the events and characters that have shaped it over the centuries.

Sir Kenneth Scott was educated at George Watson's College and the University of Edinburgh. He joined the Diplomatic Service and was posted to Moscow, Bonn, Washington, Vientiane and Brussels before being appointed Ambassador in Yugoslavia in 1982. From 1985 to 1996 he was one of the Private Secretaries to The Queen, and during most of that time he lived in an apartment in St James's Palace. In 1996, after retirement from the Royal Household, he spent nine months in Sarajevo as Chairman of the Provisional Election Commission which organised the first democratic elections in Bosnia after the war. He is the author of *St James's Palace, A History* and lives in Edinburgh.

FRONT COVER
Dalkeith Palace as designed by James Smith Kneller's Portrait of Anna, Duchess of Buccleuch and her sons
Walter Francis, 5th Duke of Buccleuch William, 6th Duke of Buccleuch
Courtesy of the Duke of Buccleuch
James Douglas, 4th Earl of Morton, 1516–1581, Regent of Scotland by Arnold Bronckhorst
General George Monck, 1st Duke of Albemarle, 1608–1670, soldier and statesman by Sir Peter Lely and studio
Scottish National Portrait Gallery
BACK COVER
Sir David Wilkie's portrait of King George IV
Courtesy of the Duke of Buccleuch

Contents

	Introduction	9
CHAPTER ONE	The Grahams	15
CHAPTER TWO	The Douglases of Dalkeith	25
CHAPTER THREE	The Regent Morton	39
CHAPTER FOUR	The later Douglasses of Dalkeith	55
CHAPTER FIVE	The Earl of Buccleuch and his daughters	65
CHAPTER SIX	Duchess Anna and the rebuilding of the Palace	79
CHAPTER SEVEN	Duke Francis, Duke Henry and Duke Charles	101
CHAPTER EIGHT	Duke Walter Francis	123
CHAPTER NINE	Duke William	143
CHAPTER TEN	The End of the Story	155
	Appendices	163
	Index	175

Introduction

The Stately Homes of England we proudly represent –
We only keep them up for Americans to rent.
Though the pipes that supply the bathroom burst,
And the lavatory makes you fear the worst,
It was used by Charles the First
(quite informally)
And later by George the Fourth
On a journey north.

Dalkeith Palace is of course not in England, and the plumbing facilities are entirely satisfactory; but in other respects it fits Noel Coward's description exactly. It is certainly a Stately Home; it is rented to Americans; and both Charles I and George IV stayed there. It was, indeed, George IV's visit which first aroused my interest in the Palace. I had walked with my family in Dalkeith Country Park and admired the William Adam stable block, the ornate twelve-sided conservatory, and Robert Adam's splendid Montagu Bridge over the North Esk, and my grandchildren had enjoyed the excellent adventure playground, (now undergoing refurbishment), but I was only vaguely aware of the Palace itself, and knew nothing of its history. It was only when I read John Prebble's book *The King's Jaunt* about George IV's historic visit to Scotland in 1822 that I discovered that the King had stayed there throughout his visit, because the Palace of Holyroodhouse in Edinburgh was in a state of dilapidation and quite unsuitable for a royal visit.

Dalkeith House, as it is now known, is perhaps the grandest of all early classical mansions in Scotland and was known throughout much of its history as Dalkeith Palace. It was built in its present form in the first decade of the eighteenth century by James Smith for Anna, first Duchess of Buccleuch, and was until the First World War a ducal seat of great magnificence, filled with fine furniture and works of art. All that has gone, and the house though still owned by the Duke of Buccleuch is now a student residence and study centre for the University of Wisconsin; but the house itself, and the earlier castle and renaissance palace which stood on this site, have a long and colourful history dating back to at least the twelfth century. Twice in its history Scotland was ruled from this place: first from 1572 to 1578 when James Douglas, fourth Earl of Morton and Regent during the minority of King James VI, used it as his principal residence and greatly expanded it, and second from 1654 to 1660 when General George Monck, Oliver Cromwell's representative in Scotland during the Commonwealth, lived here. It was used as a royal residence from time to time by James IV, James V and James VI; it was nearly purchased as a hunting estate by King Charles I just before the Civil War; it was King George IV's headquarters in 1822, and it has also been visited by Queen Victoria, by King Edward VII and by King George V when he was Prince of

Wales. This book is an attempt to trace that history and sketch the lives of the many interesting characters who have lived here.

In writing the book I have received much help and encouragement from His Grace the Duke of Buccleuch, who generously gave me permission to use material from the Buccleuch Archives and illustrations from the Buccleuch Collection. His Private Secretary, Mrs Sandra Howat, and his Archivist, Mr Crispin Powell, could not have been more helpful, and I am most grateful to them. Warm thanks are also due to Mr John Lawler of the University of Wisconsin, who during the time when he was living at Dalkeith amassed a vast quantity of documentary material about the house and grounds which he donated to the Dalkeith History Society; the Society kindly made this material available to me as well as providing some additional information, and I am most grateful to its members. I am also grateful to Dr James Macaulay for guiding my erring footsteps through the history of Scottish architecture; to Mr Peter McGowan of Peter McGowan Associates for generously allowing me to use some of the results of his research into the history of the designed landscape and the park; to Ms Patty Walters, Resident Director of Wisconsin in Scotland, for giving me access to the house itself; and to Mr Cameron Manson, Mr Iain Herbert, and staff of the Country Park, for their help. The staff of the

National Archives of Scotland, the National Library of Scotland and the Library of the University of Edinburgh have helped me greatly in my researches, and the Royal Commission for Ancient and Historical Monuments in Scotland, the Scottish National Portrait Gallery, the National Portrait Gallery and the Museum of Scotland have provided me with some of the illustrations.

Finally, I should like to thank Argyll Publishing for making this book a reality.

Kenneth Scott, December 2014

CHAPTER ONE

The Grahams

The first known inhabitants of Dalkeith Castle were the Graham family, ancestors of the Dukes of Montrose. Lands at Dalkeith and Abercorn were granted by charter to Sir William de Graham by King David I (1124–1153) in 1127.[1] Sir William's grandfather had come to England with William the Conqueror and had been given the barony of Grantham ('Graeg Ham' in the Domesday Book) from which the family name derives. It was probably Sir William who built the first castle at Dalkeith, though there may well have been some sort of fort on the site before he came: the position of the castle, on a high ridge dominating the valley of the River North Esk, made it an obvious place for fortification, and Dere Street, one of the main roads built by the Romans when they invaded Scotland, had passed close by. King David was fond of hunting, and may well have visited the site – less than five miles in direct line from Edinburgh Castle – in the course of a hunting expedition (perhaps with Sir William accompanying him).

Sir William appears as 'Sir William de Graham of Dalkeith' as a witness to a number of the King's charters, including the one which founded the Abbey of Holyrood in 1128; this indicates that he was a trusted member of the King's entourage. His son Sir Peter was styled 'of Abercorn and Dalkeith', so his principal residence may have been Abercorn Castle, which later became a

1
David I, born in 1085, had spent most of his youth at the English court: he and two of his elder brothers had fled to England in 1093 when their uncle Donald Ban ('Donalbain' in Shakespeare's *Macbeth*) seized the throne on the death of their father, Malcolm Canmore. Their sister Edith came with them, and King Henry I (1100–35) of England married her shortly after his accession. This gave David a position of considerable influence at court – he witnessed several royal acts as 'David, the Queen's brother'. His elder brothers duly succeeded to the Scottish throne after Donald Ban was deposed in 1097, and in 1113 King Henry persuaded the second of them, King Alexander I, to appoint David as 'Prince of the Cumbrians' with jurisdiction over almost the whole of Scotland south of the Forth-Clyde line. In this capacity he was in effect Henry's viceroy in the south of Scotland, and adopted many of Henry's administrative reforms. On Alexander's death he claimed the throne of Scotland, and brought with him from England a number of English knights of Norman origin, including Sir William de Graham.

Douglas stronghold, and which stood on what is now the grounds of Hopetoun House in West Lothian. Sir Peter's son, Sir Henry de Graham, was again styled 'of Dalkeith', and Dalkeith Castle was the main residence of the Grahams for the next five generations. Sir Henry was witness to several charters issued by King William the Lion (1165–1214), younger son of David I; his son, also called Henry, was recorded as being at the court of King Alexander II (1214–1249) at Berwick in 1248, and his grandson, a third Sir Henry attended – when 'well stricken in years' – the Parliament at Scone in 1286 following the sudden death of King Alexander III (1249–1286).[2] He married the heiress of the Avenel family (now extinct) and thus acquired that family's extensive lands in Eskdale and elsewhere, and the family's possessions were further increased by the marriage of the third Sir Henry's son, Sir Nicholas, to the daughter and co-heir of the Earl of Strathearn who had large estates in Northumberland. By this time Dalkeith Castle had become the centre of a vast estate; and the Grahams were major landowners and important figures at Court.

Like his father, Sir Nicholas played an important part in the troubles following the death of King Alexander III: he sat in the Parliament at Brigham (between Kelso and Coldstream) in 1290, when the Guardians of Scotland (as the joint regents were known) and a large body of clergy and nobility agreed

2
Both of Alexander III's sons had predeceased him without heirs, and his heiress was his three-year-old granddaughter Margaret, whose parents were Alexander's daughter and King Eric of Norway. The Parliament of Scone acknowledged Margaret, the 'Maid of Norway', as Queen of Scots and elected six 'Guardians' (two bishops, two earls and two barons) to rule the country pending her return from Norway.

1.1 George Barret's painting of Dalkeith Palace from the river North Esk shows how it dominates the surrounding countryside.

that Queen Margaret (then aged seven) should be married to the son and heir of King Edward I of England (then aged six). This marriage would eventually have resulted in the union of the crowns, and it had been suggested by Alexander III himself in a letter to Edward I (1272–1307). The Guardians evidently regarded it as being in the interests of Scotland: Edward was now the most powerful monarch in Europe, and a personal link with him would, it was thought, provide stability during the minority of the young Queen of Scots. Sadly, however, Margaret died later that year on her way from Norway to Scotland. This nullified the Treaty of Brigham and precipitated a crisis – there were now no fewer than thirteen claimants to the throne of Scotland, and the Guardians turned to King Edward for advice.

King Edward saw an opportunity to establish his suzerainty over Scotland, and he summoned the Guardians and the major land-owners of Scotland, including Sir Nicholas de Graham, to meet with him at Norham Castle, on the English side of the border, in May 1291. He insisted that the Scots should acknowledge him as Lord Superior of Scotland, and after some hesitation all thirteen 'Competitors', as the claimants were known, accepted the inevitable and acknowledged Edward's overlordship. There followed a lengthy period of adjudication, in the course of which the list of 'Competitors' was reduced to two: John Balliol, Lord of Galloway, and Robert Bruce, Lord of Annandale (grandfather of King Robert I), both descended from granddaughters of King David I. A panel of arbiters was then appointed, Sir Nicholas de Graham being one of those nominated by Bruce, but it was Balliol who was eventually chosen and became King in 1292.

In 1295 King Edward demanded that Scotland should provide troops for his war against France. This demand was rejected by the Scottish Parliament, who instead sent a delegation to Paris and concluded a mutual defence treaty with King Philippe IV. Since England was at war with France, King Edward regarded this as a declaration of war by Scotland, and in the spring of 1296 he amassed a large army in the north of England and summoned a number of Scottish barons, including Sir Nicholas de Graham, to Wark Castle to renew their oaths of fealty (many of the Scottish barons owned lands in England and therefore owed loyalty to Edward for their possessions there).

The first Scottish War of Independence began with an unsuccessful attack by the Scottish army on Carlisle Castle, following which the much larger English army invaded Scotland and after a fierce battle (in which a kinsman of Sir Nicholas, Sir Patrick Graham, was killed) captured the castle of Dunbar. This put a temporary end to Scottish resistance:

King John Balliol surrendered to King Edward and was stripped of his crown and sent to captivity in the Tower of London.

There followed a ten-year interregnum (1296–1306) during which King Edward took the government of Scotland into his own hands. However, Scottish resistance revived in earnest in 1297 with the battle of Stirling Bridge, when an army led by William Wallace defeated much larger English forces; but Wallace suffered a decisive defeat the following year at the battle of Falkirk, in which another of Sir Nicholas's kinsmen was killed. Sir Nicholas himself must also have fought under Wallace, because his huge estates were declared forfeit for rebellion, and before King Edward returned to England he captured and garrisoned Dalkeith Castle. In 1303 King Edward returned for another offensive, and in February 1304 the Scots surrendered. In the hope of securing the acquiescence of the Scottish nobility to his continued rule, King Edward restored their lands to many of them; Sir Nicholas had died in 1303 but his son Sir John Graham (1278–1337) regained possession of Dalkeith Castle and his other properties.

Sir John had initially been a supporter of John Balliol, but he later joined the party of Robert Bruce, Earl of Carrick,[3] who was inaugurated as King Robert I in 1306 and embarked on a guerrilla war against the English. Sir John's lands were again declared forfeit as an enemy and rebel in 1314 by King Edward II (1307–27); but were restored to him after the defeat of the English at the battle of Bannockburn. In 1320, together with two of his Graham kinsmen, Sir John affixed his seal to the Declaration of Arbroath, an eloquent affirmation of Scottish independence which concluded with the famous passage 'It is in truth not for glory, nor riches, nor honours that we fight, but for freedom alone, which no honest man gives up except with his life'.

Edward II was deposed in 1327, and succeeded by his fifteen-year-old son as Edward III (1327–77). The following year, having failed to secure Parliamentary

3
Robert Bruce, Lord of Annandale, the unsuccessful 'Competitor' in 1292, died in 1295. His son Robert was given the title of Earl of Carrick (a title still held in Scotland by the Heir to the Throne), and in 1296 he was one of the 1,500 nobles and burgesses who met at Berwick and formally recognised Edward I as King of Scots. He died in 1304, and it was his son (known to history as 'Robert the Bruce') who was crowned as King Robert I in 1306.

1.2 The Declaration of Arbroath (1320), an appeal to Pope John XXII to put pressure on King Edward II to recognise Robert the Bruce as King of Scots. It was signed, among others, by Sir John de Graham of Dalkeith.

approval for another offensive in Scotland, his representatives renounced on his behalf all claims to suzerainty over Scotland and acknowledged Robert I as King of Scots. In 1330, however, Edward III repudiated this agreement, and two years later he again invaded Scotland. Dalkeith Castle came under attack, but the English failed to capture it and Sir John remained in full possession of his lands until his death in 1337. The castle had now been in the possession of the Graham family for six generations; but the seventh generation was the last. Sir John's son, also Sir John, had no family, and with him the direct male line of the elder branch of the Graham family died out (the Dukes of Montrose are descended from the younger brother of Sir Peter de Graham). However, one of his sisters had married Sir William Douglas, known as 'the Knight of Liddesdale', and in 1341 or 1342 Sir John resigned Dalkeith in favour of his brother-in-law.

CHAPTER TWO

The Douglases of Dalkeith

Sir William Douglas, Knight of Liddesdale (1300–1353), was one of the heroes of the second Scottish War of Independence. He was a member of a junior branch of the Douglas family, and had inherited some small family estates from his father, James Douglas of Lothian; but by the time he acquired Dalkeith Castle he had become one of the most powerful magnates in Scotland. When King Edward III invaded Scotland in 1332, Sir William with a small army of tenants and kinsmen joined forces with his great-uncle Archibald, Lord of Douglas, to resist the English invasion. Sir William was taken prisoner by the English at the battle of Dornock in Dumfriesshire early in 1333, and thus escaped the carnage of the battle of Halidon Hill later that year, when the Lord of Douglas and most of the other leaders of the Scottish resistance were killed or captured. The following year he was released and allowed to return to Scotland, whereupon he again led an armed band against the English, first in Galloway with John Randolph, Earl of Moray, and then, after Randolph's capture by the English, as a leader in his own right, basing himself in lairs in Ettrick Forest and the Pentland Hills and conducting a successful guerrilla war in collaboration with Sir Alexander Ramsay of Dalhousie. His activities extended as far north as Aberdeenshire: he played a leading part in the battle of Culblean in 1335 where the Earl of Atholl, who was the chief Scottish supporter of Edward Balliol, was defeated. He then continued to consolidate his power base in the south, capturing Hermitage Castle and thus gaining control of Liddesdale in 1337. He also seized control of upper Teviotdale, and became Constable of Roxburgh Castle near Kelso.

In 1339 he went to visit King David II (1329–71), who had been sent to France for his own safety after the battle of Halidon Hill, and returned to Scotland with a party of French knights and crossbowmen to prepare the way for the King's return. When King David returned to Scotland in 1341, he rewarded Sir William with a number of grants of land, including the Barony of Dalkeith, the Lordship of Liddesdale with Hermitage Castle, and the barony of Aberdour in Fife. He also appointed him as Warden of the Middle Marches, one of the three officials responsible for the defence of the border with England. Sir William and his allies captured Edinburgh Castle, which was heavily defended by the English but which he penetrated by disguising his troops as merchants who entered the castle in haycarts. This gave him control of virtually the whole of southern Scotland. He became known as 'the Flower of Chivalry', but his reputation was tarnished by his treatment of his comrade in arms, Sir Alexander Ramsay, in 1342.

Roxburgh Castle had fallen to the English, and Sir William had several times tried unsuccessfully to recapture it. Ramsay succeeded where Sir William had failed: he drove the English from the castle, and was rewarded by being made Constable in place of Sir William, and also Sheriff of Teviotdale. Sir William, who wanted the sheriffdom for himself, was outraged; he captured Ramsay and imprisoned him in Hermitage Castle where he left him to starve to death.

In 1346 Sir William marched with King David's army into England and laid waste a large part the north-west, but was captured at the battle of Neville's Cross near Durham. He remained a prisoner in the Tower of London until 1352, when he eventually secured his release by agreeing not to impede English armies marching through Liddesdale in return for the English allowing him to retain Hermitage Castle. When King David learned of this treacherous pact he punished Sir William by granting Hermitage Castle to his distant cousin and godson, another William Douglas.[1] In 1353 the two kinsmen confronted each other in Ettrick Forest and Sir William was murdered by his godson, who then took over his estates. He was made Earl of Douglas in 1358 and lived for some years at Dalkeith Castle; the French chronicler Froissart records that he spent fifteen days as his guest 'in a castle five leagues from

1
This William Douglas was the son of Sir William's former comrade-in-arms Archibald Douglas, Lord of Douglas, who had been killed at the battle of Halidon Hill. Archibald's brother had been Sir James Douglas (known as 'the Black Douglas' because of his swarthy complexion) who was one of Robert the Bruce's most loyal followers and who had been killed in Spain in 1330 while attempting to fulfil Bruce's dying wish that his heart should be buried in the Holy Land.

Edinburgh which is called in the country Dalquest'. Sadly Froissart left no description of the castle.

Sir William had no family, and his brother Sir John had himself been murdered in 1350; so Sir William had executed a Deed of Settlement designating his nephew James as heir to his estates. James formed an alliance with the powerful Lord of Galloway, Archibald the Grim,[2] and they both remained loyal supporters of the King when the Earl of Douglas rebelled against him in 1363. The Earl of Douglas was then forced to resign his rights to the castle and lands of Dalkeith, and in 1369 James, now styled Sir James Douglas of Dalkeith and Morton (c.1335–1420) received a charter from the King confirming his inheritance and giving him the title 'Lord of Dalkeith', in return for which he bound himself and his heirs to deliver to the King 'a pair of white gloves or a silver penny at the feast of Pentecost'. He was also given, in addition to lands in Fife and Galloway, a royal licence to rebuild and repair Dalkeith Castle, and rights over the surrounding forest area.

King David II died in 1371, and as he had no progeny the throne passed to his nephew Robert, whose parents were Robert I's daughter Marjorie and her husband Walter Stewart, the hereditary High Steward of Scotland and a powerful magnate in the west of Scotland.[3] Robert (1371–90) was duly crowned as King Robert II, and from then on the royal family bore the name of Stewart or Stuart. Sir James Douglas was present at his coronation, and the new King confirmed him in the governance of Dalkeith (he was described in the charter as 'His Majesty's dear cousin') and gave him permission to found a chapel dedicated to St Nicholas. Sir James duly built the chapel just to the south of Dalkeith Castle, dedicated to the souls of King David and the members of Sir James's own family. The chapel later became a collegiate church and is now a parish church on Dalkeith High Street. Sir James also founded a hospital for the support of the poor, and another chapel, dedicated to Our Lady and St John the Baptist, within Dalkeith Castle itself. These have not survived.

In 1386 the lands of Dalkeith and Aberdour were combined in a single barony, with Dalkeith Castle as the principal seat; and three years later Sir James was granted custody of Hermitage Castle and the lands at Liddesdale and elsewhere which had belonged to his uncle Sir William. He was by now one of the richest men in the country. He accompanied Archibald the Grim on an Embassy to France, and he was one of the commissioners sent to negotiate for the inclusion of Scotland in the Anglo-French Treaty of 1384, and one of the guarantors of the treaty with England in 1390. He was married twice: first to Lady Agnes Dunbar who had been King David II's mistress and

2

Archibald the Grim was an illegitimate son of 'the Black Douglas', and thus a cousin of the first Earl of Douglas. When the latter's son was killed at the battle of Otterburn in 1388 he succeeded him as third Earl of Douglas.

3

The office of High Steward of Scotland had been hereditary since the twelfth century, when it was conferred on a Norman Knight called Fitzalan. The third High Steward adopted the surname 'Stewart'.

through whom he acquired lands in Dumfriesshire, Berwickshire and East Lothian; and secondly to King Robert II's half-sister Egidia.

As an ally of Archibald the Grim, who had succeeded his cousin as Earl of Douglas and leader of the 'Black Douglases', Sir James came under attack in 1398 from Archibald's new rival, the Earl of Angus (known as the 'Red Douglas' from the colour of his hair), an illegitimate son of the first Earl of Douglas. Angus led a series of attacks on Sir James's rich estates in Lothian and Tweeddale, including Dalkeith which was plundered. The following year Archibald negotiated a settlement which gave Angus control of Liddesdale but compensated Sir James of Dalkeith for his losses from the raids; and Sir James subsequently became a supporter of the 'Red Douglases'.

When Sir James died in 1420 he left two wills, drawn up in 1390 and 1392 (reputedly the earliest recorded wills in Scotland), and these are a striking demonstration of his wealth. His bequests included a substantial amount of jewellery, fur robes, armour for jousting and war, and a library of books on various subjects, together with a list of books he had borrowed to be returned to their owners. He left money to Newbattle Abbey and to the collegiate church of St Nicholas in Dalkeith, and his best horse and arms to the Vicar of Lasswade to pay for his funeral. He designated as his successor his son by his first marriage, also called James. This second Sir James married a daughter of King Robert III[4] and was granted, in addition to his already widespread estates, the territorial barony of Morton in Nithsdale with Mordingtoun and Whittingeham. He was also made a Lord of Parliament as Lord Dalkeith, the first to hold that title. He was one of the richest of the Scottish nobles who were obliged to pay the ransom of £40,000 for the release from prison in England of the young King James I.[5]

The second Sir James died in 1441, and was succeeded by his elder surviving son, another Sir James. This James was officially declared insane, and was placed under the guardianship of his brother-in-law James Gifford of Sheriffhall who was appointed Constable of Dalkeith Castle. During his stewardship the mad Sir James's younger brother, Henry Douglas of Borgue, sought to take over the Dalkeith lands, and even appeared in Parliament in 1445 as 'Lord of Dalkeith'; but in 1446 King James II intervened, assumed the guardianship of the third Sir James's son and heir (who was under age), and dispossessed Henry. The heir, a fourth Sir James, came into possession of the full Dalkeith estate on his father's death the following year.

The 'Black Douglases',[6] led by William, eighth Earl of Douglas (grandson of

4

King Robert II died in 1390 and was succeeded by his son as Robert III (1390–1406).

5

King James I (1406–1437) was only twelve when his father Robert III died. His elder brother David had died in suspicious circumstances and the nobles of Scotland, fearing for his safety, arranged a ship to take him to refuge in France; but the ship was captured by English pirates, who delivered him as a prisoner to King Henry V of England. He was not released until after Henry V's death in 1422. He reigned until 1437, and was succeeded by his son James II (1437–1460).

6

The long-standing family feud between the Black Douglases (descended from the 3rd Earl of Douglas, who was the illegitimate son of the 1st Earl's uncle Sir James Douglas) and the Red Douglases (descended from the illegitimate son of the 1st Earl) came to a head when the Red Douglases supported King James II in his attempt to end the power of the Black Douglases.

Archibald the Grim), had become immensely powerful throughout the south of Scotland, and the young King James II was anxious to establish his authority over them. In 1452 he invited the Earl of Douglas to dine with him at Stirling Castle, providing him with a safe conduct. After dinner the King and Douglas got into a furious argument, and the King stabbed his guest, who was then finished off by members of the King's retinue. This provoked the fury of the Earl's supporters, led by his brother who became ninth earl. The 'Black Douglases' set fire to the town of Stirling and devastated other parts of the country. Sir James Douglas of Dalkeith was a supporter of the King and of the 'Red Douglases', so Dalkeith Castle was besieged; it withstood the siege, but the town which had grown up round the castle was destroyed. In 1455 the King succeeded in crushing the Douglas rebellion, and as a reward for his loyalty Sir James was made Earl of Morton.

In 1459 he married the King's sister Joanna, who was deaf and dumb. He devoted himself to recovering his estates and restoring Dalkeith Castle, and it was probably he who built the tower portion of the castle which survives today within Dalkeith Palace. He played little part in public affairs until the accession of King James IV[7] in 1488, after which he attended Parliament frequently; in 1491 he was made envoy to France and Castile. Her also extended the church of St

2.1 Margaret Tudor.

Nicholas which had been built by his great-grandfather, adding an apse in which he and his wife (they both died in 1493) were buried and which contains their effigies.

His son John, second Earl of Morton (1466–1513), served as Ambassador to England in 1494, and when King Henry VII's daughter Margaret Tudor came to Scotland in 1503 for her marriage to King James IV she stayed with the Earl at Dalkeith Castle. (It is reported that her younger brother, the future King Henry VIII, then aged twelve, threw a tantrum on being told that the marriage would give his sister higher precedence than him at court). She arrived

7

James III (1460–1488) was assassinated in 1488 and succeeded by his eight-year-old son as James IV.

2.2 King James IV by unknown artist.

on 3rd August, and King James went to Dalkeith to greet her. Four days later she was carried on a litter to Edinburgh, where the marriage ceremony was held at the Palace of Holyroodhouse. The second Earl also entertained the Pope's Ambassador at Dalkeith in 1506. In 1504–5 oak trees from the Dalkeith woods were chopped down and taken to Newhaven to build the new seaport there, and for the construction of the *Great Michael*, flagship of the Royal Scottish navy and the largest ship in Europe at the time.

The second Earl was killed at the battle of

2.3 King James V by unknown artist.

Flodden in 1513, together with King James IV and much of the flower of Scottish nobility. He was succeeded by his son James, the third Earl, who had married in 1507 Katherine Stewart, a natural daughter of King James IV; his wife was therefore half-sister of the new King, James V (1513–1542). He suffered from some kind of physical disability and was absolved from all military service, but he enhanced the wealth of the Dalkeith estate by starting the mining of coal. The King visited him at Dalkeith twice during his boyhood, but in 1526 Morton joined the 6th Earl of

Angus in seizing guardianship of the King and holding him in confinement for two years. In 1528 another group of nobles gained control of the King; Angus was sent into exile, and several of his followers including the Earl of Morton had their estates forfeited to the Crown.[8] Later the Earl of Morton was forced to resign his title in favour of his cousin, Robert Douglas of Lochleven (whose wife had been the King's mistress).

In 1542, when King James V was only thirty, he contracted a fatal disease (thought to have been cholera) and died, only six days after the birth of his daughter who now became Mary Queen of Scots.[9] The following year the Regency Council cancelled the punishments of Angus and his friends: Angus returned from exile, and Morton and others were restored to their titles and estates. One of the prime movers in this reconciliation was Angus's younger brother, Sir George Douglas of Pittendreich, and in gratitude (and in return for a payment of two thousand pounds) the Earl of Morton agreed to the marriage of his daughter Elizabeth to Sir George's second son James. Elizabeth was the Earl's heiress, and after their marriage her husband was styled Master of Morton; he became the fourth Earl of Morton on the death of his father-in-law in 1550.

8

Under James IV's will his widow, Margaret Tudor, was made guardian to the infant James V for as long as she remained unmarried; but in 1515 she fell in love with the young Earl of Angus and married him. Custody of the King was then disputed between two groups of nobles, one favouring an alliance with England and the other an alliance with France. Henry VIII of England encouraged the pro-England party, and chose the Earl of Angus to lead it; it was the pro-French party who gained control of the king and had Angus dismissed in 1528.

9

King James V was married twice. He wanted a French bride to cement the 'Auld Alliance' with France, and his first wife was Madeleine, daughter of King Francois I of France; but she died within a few months, and in 1539 he married Marie de Guise, a noblewoman whom he had met during the negotiations for his first marriage; she was the mother of Mary, Queen of Scots.

CHAPTER THREE

The Regent Morton

By the time the infant Mary became Queen of Scots in 1542, Henry VIII of England had divorced Catherine of Aragon, broken with the Papacy and declared himself Supreme Governor of the Church of England. Fearful of the spread of this heresy to Scotland the Archbishop of St Andrews, Cardinal Beaton, established a Regency Council with himself at its head, and appointed himself Chancellor; but the Earl of Angus and his pro-English party succeeded in arresting the Cardinal, and having the Scottish Parliament appoint the Earl of Arran as Regent.[1] Arran then signed a treaty with Henry VIII, the Treaty of Greenwich, providing for Mary's betrothal to Henry's heir, the future King Edward VI. But in 1544 the Scottish Parliament repudiated the Treaty, and there followed the five-year war with England known as the 'Rough Wooing', which began with the invasion of an English army under the Earl of Hertford.

The Master of Morton and his elder brother David (who had succeeded his uncle as 7th Earl of Angus) had supported the Treaty of Greenwich, and the Master of Morton imprisoned Cardinal Beaton at Dalkeith Castle. (The Cardinal was one of the first of many prisoners held in the castle, which was locally known as the 'Lion's Den'). Morton and Angus now passed a message to Hertford that they were prepared not only to surrender to him the strategically important

1 The Earl of Arran was the eldest surviving grandson of James II's daughter Mary, and was first in succession to the throne.

3.1 James, 4th Earl of Morton.

Castle of Tantallon but also to join forces with him. However in 1546 they switched their allegiance to France (having received pensions from the French King), and in 1548 the Master of Morton was obliged to defend Dalkeith Castle against attack by an English army under Lord Grey. He was 'sore hurt on his thigh', captured and sent to England as a prisoner, and the castle was sacked. He was released and returned to Scotland in 1550, now fourth Earl of Morton; and in 1552 the Regent Arran appointed him to the Privy Council.

In 1557 Morton's brother David died, and Morton became tutor and guardian to his nephew Archibald, 8th Earl of Angus. During the latter's minority he administered the extensive Angus estates, including Tantallon, the regality of Bothwell, and the baronies of Abernethy, Jedburgh forest, and others, in addition to his own lands at Dalkeith and Aberdour and other estates as far afield as Perthshire, Lanarkshire, Dumfriesshire and Kirkcudbright. He was now one of the wealthiest landowners in Scotland. In the same year, 1557, Morton was one of the small group of Protestant nobles who met in Edinburgh and put their names to a covenant called the 'First Band of the Protestant Congregation in Scotland', undertaking to 'maintain, set forward and establish the most blessed word of God and his Congregation'; they came to be known as the 'Lords of the Congregation of Christ'. Morton was thus

3.2 An eighteenth-century portrait of Mary Queen of Scots – the so-called 'Dalkeith portrait', now at Drumlanrig Castle.

ostensibly one of the pioneers of the Scottish Reformation, but he was by no means devoted to the cause; in the words of John Knox, 'he promised to be ours but never did plainly join'.

In fact, over the next three years he seems to have alternated between support for the Reformation and loyalty to the Catholic Mary of Guise, widow of James V and mother of Queen Mary, who had succeeded the Earl of Arran as Regent. Morton was guided, as always, by his perception of where his personal interests lay rather than by any coherent policy. In the summer of 1560, however, he finally committed himself to the Reformation by signing the ratification of the Treaty of Berwick which ensured English military assistance for the reformers. He participated in the 'Reformation Parliament' which abolished papal authority in Scotland, forbade the celebration of the Mass, and authorised a new 'Confession of Faith'; and he was appointed a member of the Council of Regency following the death of Mary of Guise. He was also one of the three commissioners appointed to try to negotiate the marriage of the young Earl of Arran, son of the Regent Arran, to Queen Elizabeth I (the Queen would have none of him, and Arran was later declared insane).

Queen Mary had been sent to France and married to the Dauphin, who later became King Francois II. When her husband died in

1561 she decided to return to Scotland, and Morton wrote to her before her departure from France claiming to have been a staunch supporter of Mary of Guise and promising his loyalty. He demonstrated his allegiance by helping the Earl of Moray to restore law and order in the Borders, and in 1562 played a prominent role in the campaign against the rebellious Earl of Huntly. Having thus ingratiated himself with the Queen, he became a leading member of her Government and in 1563 was appointed Chancellor, a post of great political importance and considerable financial benefit. He entertained the Queen at Dalkeith in 1565, and when the Queen decided in the same year to marry Lord Darnley (who was a kinsman of his),[2] Morton gave the marriage his support in return for the renunciation by Darnley's mother, the Countess of Lennox, of her long-standing claim to take over from Morton the lucrative guardianship of the Angus estates. He commanded part of the royal army which drove the Earl of Moray out of the country after his rebellion in 1565, and became one of Darnley's close confidants.

Morton was deeply implicated in the plot against the Queen's Italian secretary, David Rizzio, and was present at his murder in the Queen's apartments at Holyrood in March 1566.[3] As a result he was dismissed as Chancellor and went into exile in England until the end of the year, when he and most

2
Darnley's mother, the Countess of Lennox, was the daughter of the sixth Earl of Angus by his marriage to Margaret Tudor, widow of King James IV.

3
Darnley had originally been a friend of Rizzio, but the latter was suspected by some of the Protestant nobles of being an agent of the Pope, and they persuaded Darnley that Mary was having a sexual relationship with him. When Rizzio was having supper with the Queen at Holyrood Palace, Darnley and others burst into the room, dragged him out and stabbed him to death.

of his fellow-conspirators were granted remission. He returned to Scotland and met with the Earl of Bothwell, who gave him details of a conspiracy to get rid of Darnley. Morton claimed later to have refused to participate actively in this plot, but he was undoubtedly more involved than he admitted.[4] Whatever part he played in Darnley's murder he escaped suspicion at the time, and parliament ratified his title to the earldom soon after the murder. Only Bothwell was put on trial – and acquitted by a jury packed with his own supporters. Bothwell was clearly high in the Queen's favour, and for a time Morton gave him his support, putting his signature to the 'Ainslie's Tavern Bond'.[5]

Once again, however, Morton changed sides when he saw how the wind was blowing. A month after the meeting at Ainslie's Tavern he attended a meeting of noblemen which condemned Bothwell's marriage to the Queen; he and Lord Home tried to capture Mary and Bothwell at Borthwick Castle. Next month he was among the leaders of their opponents at the battle of Carberry on 15th June, when Mary and Bothwell were defeated. Mary was taken in captivity to Lochleven Castle, home of Morton's cousin William Douglas, while Bothwell escaped abroad. Mary was forced to abdicate on 24th July, and when her son James VI was crowned at Stirling Castle at the age of thirteen months it was Morton who took the coronation oath on his behalf. The Earl of Moray, who became Regent, was in France at the time and Morton was a member of the Council of Regency which ran the country until his return. When he assumed the regency, Moray made Morton Chancellor again, and he was also appointed Sheriff of Dumbarton and High Admiral of Scotland. He commanded the vanguard of the Regent's army which finally defeated Mary at Langside after her escape from Lochleven, and he and Moray led the Scottish Commissioners at the conference convened at York by Elizabeth I of England to determine the future of Queen Mary. It was Morton who produced to this conference the famous 'Casket letters', correspondence between Mary and Bothwell which if genuine were strong evidence of Mary's complicity in the murder of Darnley.

Moray was assassinated in 1570 and his successor as Regent, the Earl of Lennox, suffered the same fate a year later. The Earl of Mar took over the Regency, but Morton was the most powerful member of the Regency Council. He continued as leader of the forces opposing the remaining supporters of Mary, and concentrated on acquiring more wealth, including the acquisition of church lands: by the time he eventually became Regent on the death of the Earl of Mar in 1572 he was described as 'the wealthiest subject that had been in the kingdom for many years'.

4
Less than a year after Rizzio's murder, Darnley's behaviour was alienating the Queen and many in her court, and she was even considering divorce. Darnley contracted some disease and one night when he had been confined in a house in Edinburgh called *Kirk o'Field* – to avoid infecting others, including his new-born son – the house was destroyed in an explosion and Darnley's body was found in the garden; he had been strangled.

5
A week after his acquittal Bothwell invited a group of nobles and prelates to supper in Ainslie's Tavern near Holyrood and persuaded them to sign a bond pledging their support for Bothwell's marriage to the Queen.

Morton's first priority as Regent was to put an end to the civil war between those loyal to King James (and himself) and the diehard supporters of Queen Mary. The most powerful of these were the Earls of Hamilton and Huntly, and with the assistance of the English Ambassador, Killigrew, Morton arranged a conference at Perth in 1573 at which it was agreed that the two earls and their followers would accept Morton as Regent, promise religious conformity, cease all support for the King's enemies, and disband their forces in return for the restoration of their lands and their rehabilitation. This settlement enabled Morton to concentrate on the subjugation of the garrison of Edinburgh Castle, the last remaining bastion of Mary's supporters. After several unsuccessful attempts to persuade the garrison to accept peace terms similar to those agreed by Hamilton and Huntly, Morton called on the English forces which had been promised by Elizabeth I and began a bombardment of the castle, which surrendered at the end of May 1573. Sir William Kirkcaldy of Grange, commander of the Castle, and three of his accomplices were hanged, and Morton was now able to govern the country peacefully for the next five years. He did so largely from Dalkeith, and a number of meetings of the Privy Council were held there.

The Mint for issuing the Scottish coinage was located in Edinburgh Castle, and while the castle was occupied by Queen Mary's supporters they continued to issue coinage bearing the Queen's image. In 1572 Morton persuaded the Privy Council to authorise the issue of silver coins bearing the King's coat of arms and superscription, and the Scottish burghs were ordered to proclaim this new coinage from their market crosses. Morton established a mint at Dalkeith Palace to produce these coins. He was accused of debasing the currency and raising prices, and his control of the coinage together with his sequestration of Church property provided him with the resources to undertake a major building project at Dalkeith, transforming the castle into 'a magnificent palace, richly adorned with tapestry and pictures, fitter for a king than a subject'. A late seventeenth-century drawing by John Slezer gives an indication of its appearance, though it includes a second outer courtyard, wall and gatehouse which were added in the seventeenth century. Morton's palace was built round a single courtyard entered from the south-east across a drawbridge and a substantial gatehouse, with buildings on all sides, including a tall turreted tower on the north-west side and an L-shaped tower on the south-west side overlooking a steep slope down to the River North Esk. This latter tower was probably part of the original castle, and the first two floors are still incorporated into the eighteenth-century building. Morton

3.3 Coin from Dalkeith Mint.

was a keen gardener – he is believed to have laid out the extensive terraced garden at Aberdour Castle in Fife, which he also greatly extended – and he is likely to have established gardens at Dalkeith. He may have been responsible for the levelling of the large area in front of the Palace: a late seventeenth century plan, on which the outline of the Palace corresponds to the Slezer drawing, shows two large parterres on either side of the main approach to the Palace. Parterres were being developed at French chateaux by the mid-sixteenth century, and it is possible that Morton was responsible for these too. To the north of the Palace, aerial photography suggests that the so-called Steel Park ('steel'

3.4 A seventeenth-century engraving of Dalkeith Palace by John Slezer; this shows the Earl of Morton's sixteenth-century palace with the additional courtyard and gateway added for the visit of King Charles I in 1637.

meaning twenty-six acres) was also under cultivation in the sixteenth century.

In the course of his rise to power and his tenancy of the Regency, Morton had made many enemies, of whom the most dangerous were the Earls of Argyll and Atholl. Morton had been in dispute with Argyll for some years over the question of some royal jewels which had come into the possession of the Argylls and which the Regent insisted should be restored to the Crown. He had also exploited for his own purposes a feud which had developed between Argyll and Atholl. But by the end of 1577 the feud had ended, and Argyll and Atholl summoned a Convention at Stirling Castle, which was attended by Sir Alexander Erskine, the King's guardian, and by the Earls of Caithness, Montrose, and Eglinton, and which used the authority of the infant King to dismiss Morton as Regent. Morton retired to his cousin's home at Lochleven.

Shortly afterwards, however, Sir Alexander Erskine was replaced as guardian to the King by his young nephew, now Earl of Mar; the latter was a supporter of Morton (his sister was married to Morton's nephew) and he strongly disapproved of his uncle's role in displacing the Regent. Morton enlisted his help and made overtures to Argyll and Atholl for a reconciliation, and with some help from Queen Elizabeth I, who exhorted the King to restore Morton to his Council, this was achieved.

Morton, Argyll and Atholl met at Dalkeith and agreed to go to Stirling together and call for a full meeting of the Council, at which Morton was not only restored to the Council but made leader of it. This was subsequently ratified by a meeting of Parliament in July 1578 – the first to be held since Morton had assumed the Regency.

Morton next launched an attack on the unpopular Hamilton family. Its two most prominent members, Lord John and Lord Claude, escaped to France but their deranged brother, the Earl of Arran, and his mother the Duchess of Chatelherault were seized and forced to hand over the Hamilton estates to the Crown. King James approved of this action, and is reported to have said that 'no nobleman's service to Scotland was to be compared to Morton's'. In October 1579 the King visited Morton at Dalkeith and was entertained 'with great honour'.

Morton's renewed ascendancy was short-lived. In 1580 there arrived from France Esme Stewart, Lord of Aubigny, who was a kinsman of the King (Lord Darnley, the King's father, was his cousin). He was handsome, charming, and accomplished, and the King was captivated by him – he was the first in a long line of male favourites of King James, who evidently had homosexual inclinations. Esme Stewart was given the Earldom of Lennox (vacant since the assassination in 1571 of his uncle, the fourth

Earl and previous Regent), and promoted to Duke of Lennox in 1581. He became a powerful figure, and a focus for Morton's enemies. He formed an alliance with Captain James Stewart, who had returned from being a mercenary in the French King's Guard and who also became a favourite of King James; it was he who, at a meeting of the Privy Council in the King's presence in 1581, accused Morton of being an accessory to the murder of Darnley. Morton was taken into custody and imprisoned first at Holyrood and Edinburgh Castle and then at Dumbarton Castle, a Lennox stronghold. In May 1581 he was brought back to Edinburgh Castle to face trial on a lengthy list of charges; but to speed up the proceedings, all of these charges were dropped except for complicity in Darnley's murder. On 1st June he was found guilty by a jury consisting almost entirely of his enemies, and the following day he was executed at Edinburgh Mercat Cross by means of the 'Maiden', a form of guillotine which he had himself imported from England. It was a fitting end to a career of treachery, violence and greed.

3.5 'The Maiden', with which the Earl of Morton was executed.

CHAPTER FOUR

The later Douglases of Dalkeith

When the fourth Earl of Morton was executed his estates were forfeited to the Crown, and his title was conferred on John, eighth Lord Maxwell, a friend of the King's favourite, the Duke of Lennox.[1] Maxwell was also granted Morton's forfeited estates, with the exception of Dalkeith and Aberdour: these were granted to Lennox, who was made Chamberlain and the King's chief minister. Lennox's ascendancy did not last long: in 1582 a group of Protestant nobles who suspected him of being a Roman Catholic seized the sixteen-year-old King in the so-called 'Ruthven raid' and took over the government of the country. Lennox was exiled and died in France soon after, and from then on Dalkeith Palace reverted to the Crown and was often used by the King himself as a residence. It was there that he received news of the execution at Fotheringay in 1587 of his mother Mary Queen of Scots, and the Privy Council met regularly at Dalkeith until 1599. His Queen, Anne of Denmark, gave birth to a daughter at Dalkeith in 1598, but the baby died soon after and royal visits became less frequent. After his accession to the English throne as James I in 1603, the King visited Dalkeith only once, during his visit to Scotland in 1617.

Meanwhile in 1586 the attainder on the fourth Earl of Morton was revoked. His wife had been declared insane early in their married life, and none of the ten children

1
The Earl of Maxwell was a grandson of the third Earl of Morton, and in 1572 he had married a sister of the 8th Earl of Angus, who was the 4th Earl of Morton's nephew and ward. The 4th Earl had been host at their wedding reception at Dalkeith Palace.

which she had borne to him survived infancy, so his nephew the Earl of Angus (1555–1588) was permitted to succeed him as fifth earl, and was appointed by the King as Lieutenant and Justiciar of the Borders.[2] Angus also succeeded to the Dalkeith estates, but in 1588 he died at Smeaton, an estate just north of Dalkeith which was to become part of the Dalkeith estate 130 years later. His death at the early age of thirty-three was popularly attributed to witchcraft, but was probably caused by tuberculosis. He too left no heir, and under the will of the fourth earl the succession passed to his cousin, Sir William Douglas of Lochleven (1540–1606), who now became sixth earl.[3]

The sixth earl's mother was Margaret Erskine, who had been one of King James V's mistresses, and he was thus half-brother to Mary Queen of Scots. He was the reluctant custodian of the Queen when, after the battle of Carberry, his castle of Lochleven was chosen as her prison. He was a close associate of his cousin the fourth earl, who had stayed with him at Lochleven after his dismissal from the regency in 1578, and of the Earl of Angus. The estates which the sixth Earl of Morton inherited were scattered over ten sheriffdoms from Angus in the north to Roxburgh in the borders; but he suffered from recurrent illness throughout his life and had to be carried in a litter when he went to visit them from Dalkeith. Despite this he lived until 1606, outliving all his four sons, and was succeeded by his eldest grandson William (1582–1648) as seventh earl.

The seventh Earl of Morton was appointed a Gentleman of the Bedchamber to King James VI of Scotland and I of England soon after succeeding to the title, and he retained this post under King Charles I. He began his political career as a member of the Convention of Estates and of the Peace Commission for Peeblesshire, Edinburgh, Fife and Kinross. He entertained King James and his retinue, which included Francis Bacon and the future Archbishop Laud, at Dalkeith during the King's visit to Scotland in 1617, and shortly thereafter, having been given special licence to travel abroad, went to France with his cousin the eleventh Earl of Angus, travelling as far as Geneva and Marseilles. On his return in 1620 he was appointed a Justice of the Peace for Edinburgh, and the following year attended Parliament and was made a Privy Councillor. In 1624 he was appointed to the Prince's Council (as an adviser to the future King Charles I) and thereafter spent much of his time at Whitehall. He was a standard bearer at the funeral of King James VI and I in 1625, and then returned to Scotland where he was reappointed to the Scottish Privy Council. He became Lord High Treasurer of Scotland in 1630, a Knight of the Garter in 1634 and Captain of the Yeomen of the Guard in 1635.

2

Maxwell still called himself Earl of Morton, and maintained the claim until his death in 1593. His elder son appeared in Parliament as Earl of Morton in 1607, in defiance of an order by the Privy Council, but was arrested and attainted. The claim was finally renounced by his brother in 1620, when he was made Earl of Nithsdale.

3

The earldom of Angus passed to a distant cousin, who was descended from the 5th Earl of Angus.

4.1 King Charles I (studio of Sir Anthony van Dyke).

King Charles I stayed with him at Dalkeith after his Coronation at Holyrood Palace in 1633 and again during a visit to Scotland in 1637, and was so attracted by the Palace that he decided to purchase it as a hunting estate. The defences of the Palace were strengthened and a second drawbridge was added; the late seventeenth-century engraving of the Palace by John Slezer (see page 50) shows the result.[4]

The Earl of Traquair, who had succeeded Morton as Lord High Treasurer in 1636, took up residence at the Palace on behalf of the King; and several meetings of the Privy Council were held at Dalkeith in 1637–38. But by this time the King was in open conflict with the Church of Scotland because of his insistence on introducing an Anglican-type Prayer Book: in 1638 thousands of Scots signed the National Covenant, pledging themselves to disregard the King's innovations and defend the reformed religion; and Charles's response was to issue a proclamation forbidding hostile demonstrations on pain of treason. The King was in fact preparing for war in Scotland, and Traquair secretly conveyed munitions to Dalkeith; the regalia of Scotland were also put there for safe keeping. In 1639 King Charles led an army to the Scottish border, but General Alexander Leslie, who had been appointed Commander of the Scottish covenanting army, forced the King to accept a truce (the 'Pacification of Berwick').[5] Leslie later captured Dalkeith Palace, expelled Traquair and restored the regalia to Edinburgh Castle. In 1642 Morton returned to the Palace, but by this time the Civil War between the King and Parliament had broken out in England, and there was no prospect of the sale of the Palace to the King being

4
When the Palace was sold to the Earl of Buccleuch in 1642 the sale included 'the castle, gardens, woods and parks of Dalkeith, with all the lands within the stone walls of the said park'. A late sixteenth-century map published by Hendrik Hortius and reproduced overleaf shows the estate as a large area between the rivers North Esk and South Esk, enclosed by a wall, and some 800 acres had been enclosed as a deer park.

5
General Leslie had served in the army of King Gustav II of Sweden and had risen to the rank of Field Marshal. The Scots invited him home to command the covenanting army, and he brought with him a number of Scottish soldiers who had served with him. After King Charles I had given in to the Covenanters in 1641 Leslie was made Earl of Leven.

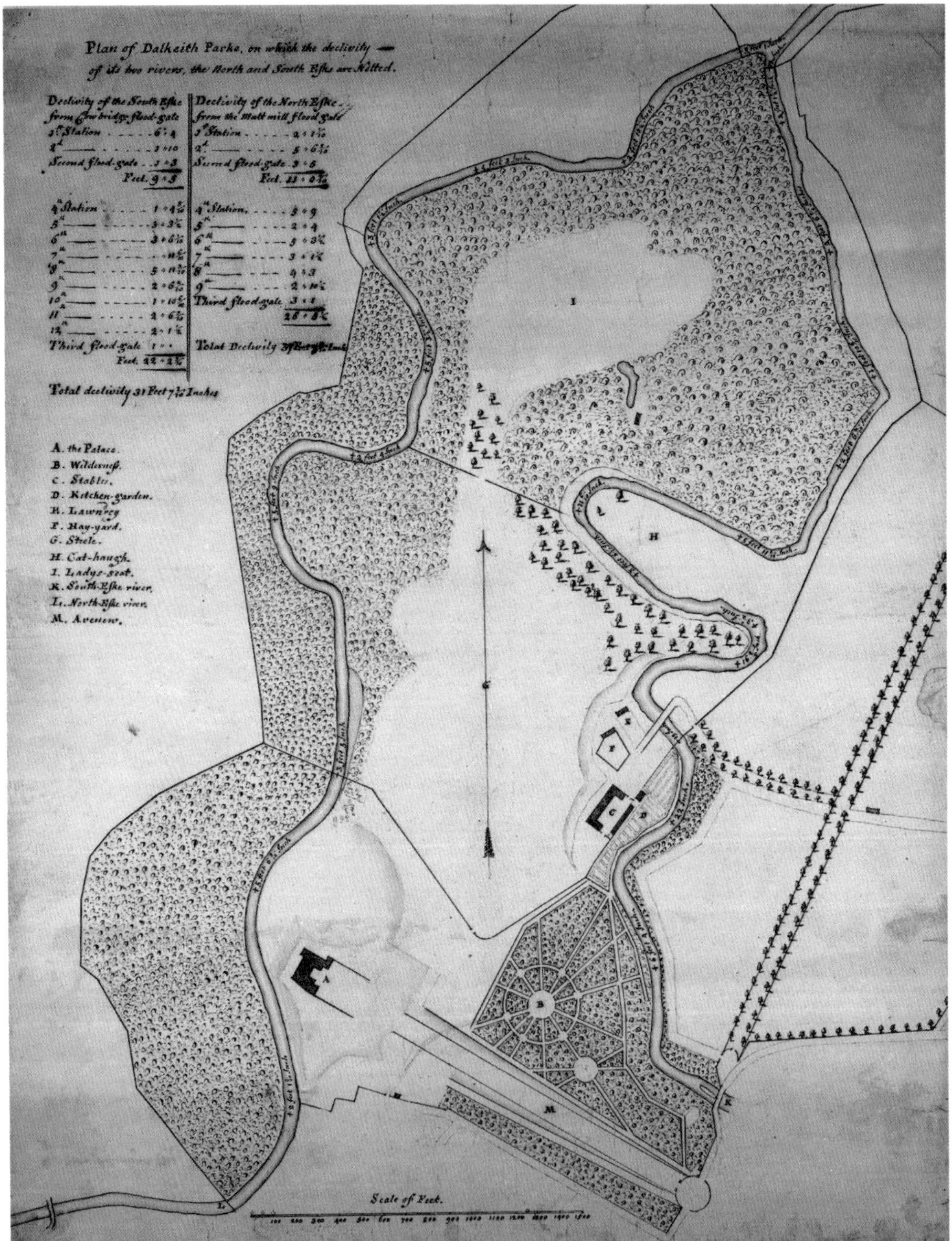
Plan of Dalkeith Parke, on which the declivity of its two rivers, the North and South Eskes are Nilted.
Declivity of the South Eske
Declivity of the North Eske
from the Malt mill flood gate
1st Station
Second flood-gate
Feet.
4th Station
Third flood-gate
Total Declivity
Total declivity 31 Feet
A. the Palace.
B. Wilderness.
C. Stables.
D. Kitchen-garden.
E. Lawnrey
F. Hay-yard.
G. Steele.
H. Cat-haugh.
I. Ladys-seat.
K. South-Eske river.
L. North-Eske river.
M. Avenew.
Scale of Feet.

completed: in the words of a new charter, 'seeing by the emptiness of His Majestie's coffers . . . and withal His Majestie considering that in respect of the great and weighty affairs for the present he cannot conveniently spare the disbursement of so great sommes of money, therefore His Majestie dispones to the said William Earl of Morton the lands and lordship of Dalkeith.' Having contributed a large part of his fortune to help finance the Royalist Army, the Earl of Morton was obliged to put the Palace and some of his other estates (to a value of £100,000 Scots of yearly rent) up for sale. He was heavily in debt to (amongst others) Francis Scott, second Earl of Buccleuch, and it was to him that he sold Dalkeith for £500,000 Scots.

4.2 A 1639 map of the Dalkeith estate published by Hendrick Hortius.

CHAPTER FIVE

The Earl of Buccleuch and his daughters

Francis, second Earl of Buccleuch (1626–51), the new owner of Dalkeith Palace, was the head of one of the principal families of the Scottish borders.

His grandfather, Walter Scott (known to history as 'the bold Buccleuch') was famous for his daring raid on Carlisle Castle in 1596 to rescue the notorious Border reiver 'Kinmont Willie' who had been captured by the English;[1] but Buccleuch himself had abandoned the family tradition of border raiding and feuding with his neighbours, and he gave his support to King James VI who, as the prospect of becoming James I of England drew nearer, embarked on a campaign to pacify the Borders. Walter Scott was knighted by the King in 1590 and appointed Keeper of Liddesdale and Warden of the Western Marches; and in 1594, as a reward for his 'good, faithful and thankful service . . . in pacifying the Borders and middle Regions of the Marches', the King granted him by charter most of the estates forfeited by his stepfather, the fifth Earl of Bothwell.[2] These estates were scattered across the Borders from Dumfriesshire to Berwickshire, and their acquisition by Buccleuch made him one of the major landowners in Scotland. In 1606 he was made Lord Scott of Buccleuch. His son, also called Walter, succeeded in 1611 and was made Earl of Buccleuch in 1619. He spent over a quarter of a million pounds on buying even more land and went heavily into

1
William Armstrong of Kinmont ('Kinmont Willie') had been captured by English troops in 1596 while he was protected by a safe conduct, attending a murder trial as a witness, and imprisoned in Carlisle Castle. The 'bold Buccleuch', on whose land this breach of the law had occurred, petitioned the commander of the castle to release him, and when this request was refused he broke into the castle with a body of armed men and freed Armstrong. Queen Elizabeth I was outraged, and demanded that Buccleuch should be arrested and sent to London. There he was received by the Queen, who asked him how he dared attack one of her castles. When Buccleuch replied 'What is it that a man dare not do?' the Queen was impressed and is said to have remarked 'with ten thousand such men, our brother in Scotland might shake the firmest throne in Europe'. Buccleuch was released.

2
The fifth Earl of Bothwell was a nephew of the Bothwell who married Mary Queen of Scots. He was an inveterate plotter against King James VI, and was charged with treason in 1594 and fled into exile in France.

debt, but with the help of his kinsman Sir William Scott of Harden was able to clear most of his debts by the time of his death in 1633. However, by that time King Charles I, who acceded to the throne in 1625, had decreed that Buccleuch should surrender one-third of the Bothwell estates to Bothwell's son. This led to a prolonged negotiation, which ended only in 1647 when the Earl of Buccleuch received a charter for the other two-thirds of the Bothwell estates on the payment of £50,000.

Francis, the second Earl, was only seven when he succeeded to the title in 1633. He was living with his aunt Margaret, Lady Ross, at Melville Castle near Dalkeith, his mother having died in childbirth two years before her husband. Eight members of the extended Scott family were designated in his father's will as his 'tutors' (i.e. guardians), and they sent Francis and his brother David to St Andrews University in 1636 when Francis was ten and David nine. Francis stayed at St Andrews until 1643 (apart from a brief appearance in Parliament in 1641) and by then the Scottish and English Parliaments had agreed a 'Solemn League and Covenant' under which the Scots would send an army into England to fight with the Parliamentary forces against King Charles I, and the English would guarantee the preservation of the Presbyterian settlement in Scotland. Francis left university and raised a regiment from his estates, with himself as colonel, which joined the large Scottish army and crossed the border playing a crucial role in the storming of Newcastle and the defeat of the Royalist forces at the battle of Marston Moor in 1644.

In 1646, at the age of nineteen, he was appointed to the Committee of Estates which acted as the government of Scotland when Parliament was not in session, and in the same year he married Margaret Leslie, sister of the Earl of Rothes and widow of Lord Balgonie (son of the covenanting General Alexander Leslie).

The Earl and Countess began their married life at Dalkeith Palace, which was the grandest of the Buccleuch residences and which Francis clearly intended to replace Branxholm Castle in Teviotdale as the principal family seat. They had four children: Mary, born in 1647, Walter (1648), Margaret (1650) and Anna (1651); but Walter and Margaret both died in infancy. The Earl was becoming more involved in active politics: in 1647 he was one of the minority of Covenanting aristocrats who opposed the decision to change sides and attempt to restore Charles I to freedom after his defeat in the Civil War. The Scottish army once more moved into England, but was defeated by Cromwell at the Battle of Preston in 1648. When Charles I was executed in 1649, Buccleuch, together with his uncle the Earl of Eglinton, joined with the Earl of Argyll in arranging for the King's elder son to be proclaimed as King Charles II in Edinburgh, and he was a member of the committee sent to welcome the new King when he came to Scotland in 1650. Oliver Cromwell, now Lord Protector of the Commonwealth, responded by invading Scotland and defeating the Scottish army at Dunbar, and the Countess of Buccleuch took her children to safety in Dundee, where Anna was born. The most valuable contents of the Palace were sent to the Bass Rock, off the coast of East Lothian, for safe keeping; but what remained at the Palace was plundered by Cromwell's troops.

General George Monck, a close friend and supporter of Cromwell, was left in charge of the Parliamentary forces in Scotland when Cromwell pursued Charles II into England, and he proceeded to attack a number of royalist strongholds in Scotland including Dundee; so the Buccleuch family moved first to Aberdeen and then to the Earl of Rothes's Leslie House in Fife. They were able to return to Dalkeith in October 1651, and it was there that the Earl of Buccleuch died the following month, at the age of only twenty-four, after making a will designating his elder daughter Mary as heiress to his title and estates and appointing a number of members of the Scott family as tutors to his daughters.[3]

By the end of 1651 Scotland was under English military occupation. At the beginning of 1652 the Scottish Parliament was dissolved,

5.1 General George Monck.

and the Privy Council was replaced by a 'Commission for Settling and Managing the Affairs of Scotland', appointed by the English Parliament. The Commissioners chose Dalkeith Palace as their headquarters (perhaps in the mistaken belief that it was Crown property),

3
The Earl of Buccleuch was buried in the sacristy of St Nicholas' Church, founded 400 years earlier by Sir James Douglas (see Chapter 2); the sacristy had been walled off from the rest of the church at the time of the Reformation, when it was regarded as a 'monument of idolatry'. It had been used for a time as a prison, and later became the family vault in which several generations of the Buccleuch family are interred. The infant son of General George Monck was also buried there.

and took up residence there in January 1652. The widowed Countess of Buccleuch and her two surviving daughters were obliged to move to Sheriffhall House, a mansion on the Dalkeith estate less than two miles from the Palace. Colonel Robert Lilburne, who replaced Monck as Commander of the army in Scotland in 1652 when Monck fell ill, lived at Dalkeith Palace until Monck returned in 1654. Monck then became the virtual ruler of Scotland: as Commander-in-Chief he was given power to collect taxes, impose fines and imprisonment, and issue proclamations. He used these powers to suppress all opposition to Parliamentary rule, and introduced a period of greater stability than the country had known for many years.

From 1654 to 1659 Dalkeith Palace was the virtual seat of government for Scotland, and Monck and his wife lived there in some state. He occupied his spare time in planting a large number of trees in the park (there is an avenue near the Palace still known as 'General Monck's walk') to replace the large number cut down by Colonel Lilburne and transported to Leith for shipbuilding. Monck paid a rent to the Buccleuch estates for the park and orchard, together with a token amount for the Palace itself.

Earl Francis's widow, a lady of strong character who knew exactly what she wanted and usually got it, soon found herself a new husband, and in January 1653 she was married at Sheriffhall to the second Earl of Wemyss, after which she and her daughters moved to Wemyss Castle in Fife. The elder daughter, Mary, was now Countess of Buccleuch in her own right and owner of the vast Buccleuch estates, and a number of Scottish nobles were hoping to marry her off to one of their sons. Among these was her uncle the Earl of Tweeddale, whose wife Jean (sister of Earl Francis) was next in succession to the Buccleuch earldom after the two little girls. Tweeddale was heavily in debt to the Buccleuch estates, and he soon tried to persuade the tutors to remove the children from their mother's control.[4] The mother was determined that Tweeddale should not succeed, and Lord Wemyss on his wife's behalf travelled to London and petitioned the Lord Protector to support her request to the tutors to be allowed to retain custody of the children until they were twelve; Cromwell agreed, and this recommendation was passed to the tutors, who eventually accepted it. So it was agreed that Mary would remain in the custody of her mother until 1659 when she would be twelve years old, at which age she could legally be married.

Lady Wemyss had an ally among the tutors in the person of Sir Gideon Scott of Highchester, son of her late husband's close adviser Sir William Scott of Harden. It was agreed between them that Sir Gideon's son Walter would be a suitable husband for Mary,

4
Under Scottish law a widow's right to custody of her children expired when they were seven years old; Mary would reach this age in 1654.

thus removing the threat of a marriage to Tweeddale's son. In January 1659 Lord Wemyss invited Sir Gideon to bring his son, a fourteen-year-old student at St Andrews, for a few days to Wemyss Castle. The two young people took a liking to each other, and it was agreed that they should be married as soon as possible. The presbytery of Kirkcaldy was persuaded by Lord Wemyss to dispense with the normal period of three weeks during which the banns of marriage should be proclaimed, and the marriage took place in February, when Mary was seven months short of her twelfth birthday. Tweeddale and a number of the tutors at once sent a petition to General Monck claiming that the marriage was illegal and should be annulled, and asking that both Mary and Anna should be removed from their mother's custody. Monck referred the petition to the commissioners who had replaced the Court of Session, and they decided that Mary should be placed in the custody of a third party until she reached the age of twelve. Lady Wemyss objected to all the custodians proposed by the Commissioners, and instead suggested that Mary should be looked after by General Monck himself at Dalkeith Palace, her family home. No one could object to this ingenious solution, and Mary lived at Dalkeith with Monck and his wife until after her twelfth birthday, when the marriage was authenticated and the young couple were reunited at Wemyss Castle.

5.2 King Charles II (studio of John Riley).

General Monck was now to play a key role in the restoration of King Charles II. The King had written to him in 1655, and he had at once sent a copy of this letter to Cromwell, who jokingly replied saying 'There be those that tell me that there is a certain cunning fellow in Scotland called George Monck who is said to lie in wait there to introduce Charles Stuart; I pray you, use your diligence to apprehend him and send him up to me'. When Cromwell died in 1658 Monck transferred his loyalty to his son and successor Richard Cromwell, to whom he sent from Dalkeith a private letter of advice. But in the spring of 1659 the army in England deposed Richard and recalled Parliament, and although Monck was confirmed in charge of affairs in Scotland his relationship with the new regime in London became strained. In the summer of 1659 the exiled King Charles, seeing an opportunity to enlist Monck's support, sent Sir John Grenville, who was the King's Lord of the Bedchamber and a cousin of Monck, to Dalkeith together with Monck's younger brother Nicholas with a letter to Monck (signed 'Your affectionate friend Charles R') introducing Grenville as having authority to offer Monck 'such an estate in land, and such a title of honour as he himself shall desire, if he will declare for me and adhere to my interest'. The King told Monck that he left it to his own judgement how he would declare his allegiance, and promised to comply with his advice.

Monck did not respond immediately to this approach; but he became increasingly disillusioned with the Parliament and in September he offered his resignation to the Speaker of the House of Commons, who refused to accept it. Monck continued to profess his loyalty to the Parliament, and when the English army expelled the Parliament in October 1659 he decided to mobilise his forces in Scotland to oppose them. He now replied to the King's offer with a letter from Dalkeith in which he described the 'sad and lamentable condition' of the country as being 'occasioned for want of its ancient and ever accustomed way of government, to wit, a King and Parliament'. He claimed to have the power to bring about the restoration of the monarchy, and proposed that the King should consent to a treaty between himself and a free Parliament (excluding any involved in or profiting from the execution of Charles I), should declare what mercy he was prepared to show to his enemies 'upon their submission and promise of future obedience', and should promise satisfaction to the 'poor common soldiery who were forced to take up arms against Your Majesty for sheer necessity to keep them and their families from starving'. He added that he would 'carry as fair a correspondence as I can' with the Parliament and Army in London and intended shortly to go to London to see how things now stood; and he requested a speedy reply to his letter.

By December Monck had remodelled the army in Scotland into a force loyal to himself, and he marched south, arriving in London in February 1660; there he arranged new parliamentary elections and began the process which led to the restoration of the monarchy. In April the King issued the Declaration of Breda, which was based on the advice Monck had given him, and in May the King arrived at Dover where Monck was the first to greet him (and was duly rewarded with the Dukedom of Albemarle).

Following Monck's departure from Scotland, Dalkeith Palace remained unoccupied by the family for forty years, and the Buccleuch estates were managed by a succession of curators, of whom the most prominent was George, Lord Melville, whose wife was a daughter of Lady Wemyss by her second marriage and thus step-sister to the Buccleuch heiresses. Countess Mary continued to live with her husband and her mother and stepfather at Wemyss Castle; but she had for some time been suffering from a painful disease (thought to have been bone cancer) and she enjoyed less than two years of marriage before she died in the spring of 1661. The Buccleuch title and fortune then passed to her sister Anna now aged ten, and once again there was keen competition among her relatives to produce a husband for her. This time it was another uncle, the Earl of Rothes (Lady Wemyss's brother), who made the first move: he persuaded the Earl of Lauderdale, now Secretary of State, to seek the King's approval for the appointment of Rothes as Anna's guardian, and the King so decreed only ten days after Mary's death. Lady Wemyss was taken by surprise, and she appealed to Monck; but Monck refused to help her, and there now seemed to be a real danger that Rothes, in return for a substantial payment by Lord Tweeddale, would gain the approval of the tutors for Anna's marriage to the latter's son, Lord Yester. Lady Wemyss was determined to prevent this, and thought of a brilliant solution: she wrote to King Charles proposing Anna as a husband for the King's eldest and favourite illegitimate son James Crofts (who had taken his surname from his guardian Lord Crofts, a Gentleman of the Bedchamber). The King accepted this proposal with delight, and in June 1662 Lady Wemyss and her daughter went to London.

Tweeddale and his supporters tried to prejudice the Court against Anna, describing her of being 'of low stature, weakness and infirmities of body, and uncomelinesse' but Sir Gideon described her at that time as being 'a proper, handsome, and a lively tall young lady', and King Charles was duly impressed. The following month young James Crofts, aged thirteen, was brought to London by his guardian and entered London society where he was described by Samuel Pepys in his diary as 'a most pretty spark'. The King made him Duke of Monmouth in November, and a marriage contract was drawn up which provided that, if Anna were to die childless, the Buccleuch estates would pass to Monmouth, who in compliance with the Buccleuch entail adopted the surname of Scott. He and Anna danced together at the New Year's Eve ball, and Pepys thought Anna one of the best of the dancers; and in April 1663 the marriage was celebrated in the Palace of Whitehall. The King marked the

5.3 The Duke of Monmouth.

occasion by appointing them Duke and Duchess of Buccleuch as well as of Monmouth.

It was not a happy marriage. They had seven children, of whom only three, two sons and a daughter, survived childhood; but the young Duke had inherited his father's sexual appetites, and Pepys wrote that he spent his time viciously and idly, 'whoring and rouging of it'. A Tuscan visitor to the Court reported in 1667, when he was eighteen, that he had already had several bouts of venereal disease. He was spoiled by the King, who lavished money on him; and although he had good looks and great charm, and distinguished himself as a soldier, he was shallow and unintelligent. He and Anna had no interests in common except dancing, and even this pleasure was denied to Anna when in 1668 she fell while dancing, dislocated her hip, and was lame for the rest of her life. She and her husband lived apart for much of their married life: Monmouth was sent off to serve in the Royal Navy under his uncle the Duke of York during the Second Anglo-Dutch War in 1665, and again in command of a brigade in the Third Anglo-Dutch War in 1672–73. Back home in 1674 he set up house with a woman called Eleanor Needham, who bore him three children, and in 1678–9 he was again away from home, first commanding an Anglo-Dutch brigade fighting against the French and then, having been appointed Commander-in-Chief, going to Scotland to

defeat the Covenanters at the Battle of Bothwell Bridge.

Meanwhile Anna was left alone, either in their house in Soho or at their country home, Moor Park in Hertfordshire, which the King had bought for them in 1670: her mother had returned to Scotland in 1663, having tried unsuccessfully to persuade the King to let Anna go with her. The Duchess was a great favourite at Court, particularly with the

Duchess of York (wife of the future King James II) with whom she travelled to Holland in 1668 to visit the Princess of Orange, the future Queen Mary II. Anna was a great deal more intelligent than her husband: the diarist John Evelyn described her as being 'one of the wisest and craftiest of her sex', and another courtier wrote that 'her mind possessed all those perfections in which the handsome Monmouth was so deficient'. She took an interest in the arts, and before she went lame she acted in a number of plays at court; she was an admirer of John Dryden, who described her as his 'first and best Patroness'; and she was a patron of Sir Godfrey Kneller, from whom she took painting lessons. Kneller painted a portrait of her with her two sons, James Earl of Dalkeith (born 1674) and Henry (born 1676), who was made Earl of Deloraine by Queen Anne in 1706.

In 1680 Monmouth fell in love with Lady Henrietta Wentworth, and went to live with her in her family home in Bedfordshire. Anna's health began to suffer from the strain and she obtained the King's permission to go to Paris with her children (and thirty servants) to recover. From there she wrote to Lord Melville asking him to continue as her principal agent for her Scottish estates, and concluding: 'I have been very ill of late. If I die, be kind to my children'. She returned to Court in 1682, and continued to live in England until 1701.

5.4 Kneller's portrait of Anna, Duchess of Buccleuch with her sons, the Earls of Dalkeith and Deloraine.

Monmouth was suspected of involvement in the 'Rye House Plot' of 1683, a plan by members of the Whig party (who were strongly opposed to the possibility of a Roman Catholic monarch) to assassinate the King and the Duke of York because of their Catholic sympathies. His appointment as Commander-in-Chief was cancelled, and he went into hiding, but Anna persuaded him to sign a confession, and the King pardoned him;

Monmouth then retracted his confession and his father, calling him a 'blockhead', banished him from Court. He and Anna lived together for a while at Moor Park, but Monmouth soon went into exile in Holland, where he remained until after his father's death in 1685.

Away from his wife's restraining influence, and egged on by Whigs by whom he was surrounded, he then decided to claim the throne for himself, and raised a rebellion against the new King James II. He landed in Dorset with three ships, denounced the King, and had himself crowned in Taunton, but his small force was soundly defeated by the King's army at the Battle of Sedgemoor. Monmouth escaped, disguised as a shepherd, but two days later he was captured and sent to the Tower of London. The King, fearing that his children might be used by the rebels, sent them to the Tower too, and Anna joined them there; her daughter Anne died in the Tower at the age of ten. When Monmouth was condemned to death, Anna visited him shortly before his execution, and was later able to convince the King that she had had no knowledge of her husband's plot. Monmouth's titles and estates were forfeited to the Crown, but Anna was granted a charter confirming her own title as Duchess of Buccleuch with all that went with it.[5]

In 1688 Anna married again, to Lord Cornwallis, and they had three children (only one of whom survived childhood). He helped her with the management of her estates in Scotland, and in 1692 they jointly signed a charter appointing Lord Melville's son Lord Leven (who was Governor of Edinburgh Castle) as her agent ('Baillie') at Dalkeith, a post which he held until Anna returned to Scotland. In 1698 Lord Cornwallis died; he had been much in favour with King William III, but Anna's particular friend Queen Mary II had died in 1694 and Anna's position at court was therefore more tenuous. So in 1701, at the age of fifty-four, she decided to return to Scotland.

5
Lord Melville, the Duchess's agent at Dalkeith, was suspected of involvement with Monmouth in the 1683 'Rye House Plot', and was obliged to go into exile; he went to Holland and attached himself to the court of William of Orange. In Melville's absence Dalkeith Palace was rented to an advocate named James Graham, who was Anna's legal adviser in Scotland. According to the overseer of the estate, Graham turned part of the Palace into a brewery, kept his wife's horses and cattle in the deer park, left the barbican door open so that schoolboys could climb on to the roof and damage the leads, and allowed his servants to hang drying lines to the chandeliers, causing them to crash to the ground. When she learned of this Anna wanted to prosecute Graham, but was dissuaded by Lord Melville, who had returned to Britain when William of Orange became King William III after the 'Glorious Revolution' of 1688. The Duchess later initiated a lawsuit against Melville himself, which dragged on for several years.

CHAPTER SIX

Duchess Anna and the rebuilding of the Palace

Duchess Anna was in her fifties when she returned to Scotland to look after her estates there. Having spent much of her life at Court during the reigns of her father-in-law Charles II, her uncle James II and her cousins William III and Mary II, she regarded herself very much as a member of the Royal Family and she was determined to convert Dalkeith Palace into a suitably royal residence. She spent the summer of 1701 in Scotland, staying for part of the time with Lord Melville at Melville House in Fife, which had recently been built by James Smith, the foremost Scottish architect of his day. Smith was Surveyor of the Royal Works, and had also designed Hamilton Palace (now demolished) for the Duke of Hamilton and rebuilt Drumlanrig Castle for the first Duke of Queensberry, whose granddaughter was to marry the second Duke of Buccleuch, Duchess Anna's grandson, and unite the two dukedoms. When Duchess Anna was planning the reconstruction of Dalkeith Palace, therefore, it was natural that she should choose James Smith as her architect.

Smith had studied architecture in Italy and had travelled elsewhere in Europe, and he played a key role in the reintroduction of Italianate architecture in Scotland, where it had fallen out of fashion in the seventeenth century. His original design for Dalkeith Palace was Palladian in style, but would have involved demolishing virtually the whole of

the existing building, and was rejected by the Duchess. A later plan, which was adopted, incorporated a good deal of the structure of the old palace. As shown in the Slezer engraving (page 50), the old palace had two courtyards, the outer one being the result of the addition of a second gateway and drawbridge on the east side[1] as part of the strengthening of the fortifications for King Charles I. Both the walls on the east side were demolished, but the sixteenth century walls of the Regent Morton's palace were retained on the south and west sides; the north wall, which dates from the seventeenth century (and was presumably also part of the

6.1 The Palace as it was designed by James Smith.

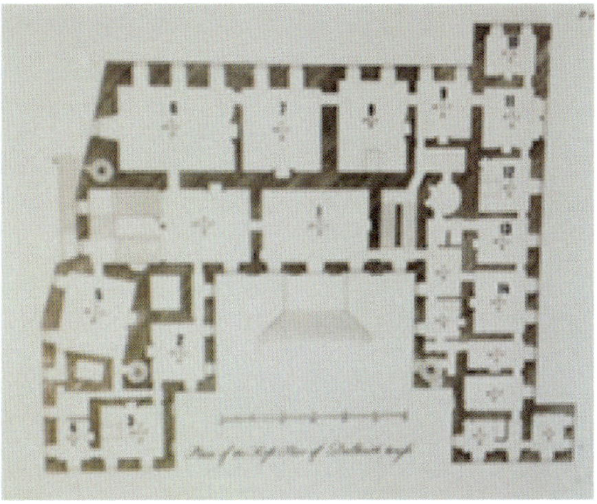

6.2 Ground floor plan of Dalkeith Palace. the room numbered 5 is the base of the fifteenth-century tower.

reconstruction for Charles I) was also retained. The south wing, from which the ground slopes steeply down to the river, incorporates the original fifteenth-century tower, and is slightly splayed except where it was brought into line for the windows of the new staircase. Smith designed an entirely new east front, with a second suite of rooms in front of the original west suite and with projecting wings to north and south of a central forecourt. The attached floor plan show the result.

The new east front, of buff-coloured sandstone from the quarries of Culross and Queensferry, gives an air of ducal grandeur to the palace. The main entrance is at the centre of a portico, and is flanked by two pairs of gigantic Corinthian pilasters surmounted by a pediment carved with the Buccleuch coat of arms.

1
The Palace faces south-east, but for simplicity it is described in this book as facing east.

6.3 William of Orange's palace of Het Loo in the Netherlands.

John Macky, in his *Journey through Scotland* published in 1729, described it as being 'the very model of King William's Palace at Loo', and some sources claim that the Duchess had actually instructed Smith to follow the design of this palace, now known as Het Loo at Appledorn in the Netherlands. There are certainly considerable similarities. Het Loo was built in 1684–86, and a description of it, published by Walter Harris in 1699, may well have been read by the Duchess (who had been a close friend at Court of William's Queen, Mary II) or by Smith himself.

The interior of the Palace is equally grand. The entrance hall, like that at Het Loo, is paved with black and white marble, and the walls are richly panelled with oak and surmounted with a painted frieze depicting cupids engaged in various activities, including apparently a game of leapfrog. A door to the left gives access to the Marble

Hall to the south, which has the same marble floor and a grand marble staircase screened by an arcade of white and grey marble. ('You will think me extravagant in marble', wrote the Duchess to Lord Melville, 'but it is to show you I do not despise my old castle'). To the west of this second hall, in the south-west corner of the palace, is the Dining Room, formerly known as the Great Antechamber; its thick walls show that it is part of the old palace, and it too is oak-panelled with a marble fireplace.[2] The Dining Room is the first of an enfilade of four state rooms, all facing west, which lead to another suite of private apartments on the north side, including the Duchess's bedroom and sitting room and the Library; this progress through ante-rooms to state apartments to private apartments echoes, no doubt deliberately, the traditional arrangement in royal palaces. In the south-east wing is the Smoking Room (formerly the Steward's Hall), a large square room with a vaulted stone ceiling – the base of the fifteenth-century tower – and three other rooms. The first floor is dominated by the Gallery – the largest room in the house – which is immediately above the entrance hall. Above the Smoking Room, and also part of the original tower with thick walls, is the Charter Room: this is where important family archives were kept, and is probably where the regalia of Scotland and the armaments were stored by the Earl of Traquair shortly before

2
It was in the Dining Room that General Monck is reputed to have conducted the correspondence which led to the Restoration of King Charles II.

the Civil War. Above the Dining Room is the principal guest bedroom, used by King George IV and later by Queen Victoria; next to it is a Drawing Room and then the bedroom used by General Monck. The remaining bedrooms and dressing rooms on the first floor could all be accessed from two servants' rooms with spiral staircases, one in the south-east wing and the other behind the suite of rooms on the north side. The second floor contained servant's quarters, and in the basement were the kitchen and other services.

Once Smith's design had been approved by the Duchess, work on the new building started quickly. The masonry contract was signed in March 1702, by which time the demolition of the old east wing was presumably completed, and the main fabric of the house was finished by the autumn of 1705 when the whole roof was slated. James Smith was himself a skilled stonemason, and he employed two cousins, James and Gilbert Smith, to assist with the stonework. Most of the marble came from Rotterdam, and it includes several chimney-pieces carved by Grinling Gibbons; the marble staircase is believed to have been the work of another London marble-cutter, Richard Neale, who with a team of assistants spent fifteen months at Dalkeith, finishing his work early in 1711. In 1704 the Duchess's chamberlain, Benjamin Robinson, and a skilled local joiner, William Walker, had travelled to London where, in the company of the Duchess's cabinetmaker James Moore, they visited a number of houses including Hampton Court Palace and Buckingham House (later to become Buckingham Palace), to look at staircases and furniture; and between 1701 and 1707 large quantities of chimneypieces, furniture, pictures, hangings, looking glasses and other fittings were shipped from London to Dalkeith. Some of these came from the Duchess's home at Moor Park, which she retained until 1720, and some from her London house in Soho, but most were specially purchased for Dalkeith; some pieces of furniture were made locally, including some by an Edinburgh cabinetmaker called William Scott. A visitor to the palace in 1732 described it as being 'furnished with the most costly elegance'.

The Duchess, however, was not satisfied with Smith's work: she made numerous complaints in 1715–6 about the quality of the masonry work, and when Smith claimed that he had not been paid in full she petitioned the Lords of Council, stating that 'I found his workmanship of my house to be in many respects defective': the chimneys smoked, the walls were sunk and cracked, the arch in her closet had sunk, and several lintels of doors and windows were cracked – 'all of which is to be imputed to the insufficiency of the work, for which the undertaker of the building is liable in damage'. In his response, Smith maintained that these defects 'could not all be charged upon the workmanship, but rather upon the foundation, which was none of his choosing'; in other words, it was the Duchess's insistence on retaining as much as possible of the old building that had caused the problems. One of his masons testified that he had previously worked on the old building, and that the chimneys had smoked then. Smith also said 'he does heartily wish that the Duchess herself had been upon the place' (she had by this time returned to London); 'in that case he was very sure that there had been no such information given'. In 1717 the Lords of Council found it proven that the work had been properly carried out, and the Duchess had to pay up.

Duchess Anna lived in the Palace for a while in some state. Her contemporaries called her 'a most formidable person', and Dr Samuel Johnson described her as being 'remarkable for inflexible perseverance in her demand to be treated as a princess'. In some legal documents she was designated 'the High and Mighty Princess Anne Duchess of Buccleuch'. When she dined she sat under a canopy, served by pages on bended knee, while all of her guests (unless they were close members of her family) were obliged to remain standing. In the local community she was regarded as an excellent employer; she provided financially for workers on the estate who were in need of help and had good housing built for them, including the miners at the coal mines which she owned at Cowden, Sherriffhall and Newbattle. But once the Palace was completed she spent little time there, preferring the life at Court in London both during the reign of Queen Anne and after the accession of King George I. According to Cowper she was a close friend and frequent guest of the future Queen Caroline (wife of George II) when Princess of Wales, and even in her sixties was described as having 'all the life and fire of youth; it was marvellous to see that the many afflictions she had suffered had not touched her wit and good nature'.

Her elder son James, the first of the family to bear the courtesy title of Earl of Dalkeith, may never even have visited the Palace, since he died at his home in London in 1705 at the early age of thirty, having spent some years fighting for King William III in Flanders.[3] James had been married in 1694 to Lady Henrietta Hyde, daughter of the Earl of Rochester, and they had four sons and two daughters. He was succeeded as Earl of Dalkeith by his eldest son Francis, who in due course became the second Duke. When the Duchess returned to London she was advised on the management of her Scottish estates by the Earl of Cromartie and more particularly by his son Sir James Mackenzie, who became a Judge of the Court of Session with the title of Lord Royston. She gave Royston a life rent

3
In 1692, when the Earl of Dalkeith was seventeen, thirty or forty 'wyld people' who had been supporters of his father the Duke of Monmouth assembled at the cross in Sanquhar in Dumfriesshire and proclaimed him King; their leader was arrested and imprisoned.

on Riddle's Court, a house she had bought in the Lawnmarket in Edinburgh, and with his help she greatly expanded the extent of the Dalkeith estate to the north-east. She bought the neighbouring property of Smeaton House in 1710 from Sir James Richardson, in whose family it had been since before the Reformation (it had originally belonged to Dunfermline Abbey), and had it rebuilt by William Adam; it was renamed East Park, and appears in Adam's *Vitruvius Scoticus.* She added most of the regality of Musselburgh in 1725. She also increased her holdings in the borders by buying the lands and lordship of Melrose in 1722. In the immediate vicinity of the Palace she had new avenues laid out, new

6.4 Smeaton House, later known as East Park.

walls and gates to the park built, and a new garden planted in place of the formal parterres which had previously stood in the forecourt. Daniel Defoe, who visited Dalkeith in 1724 in the course of his *Tour through the Whole Island of Great Britain*, saw 'fine avenues, some already made and planted, others designed but not yet finished', and he was told of plans to lay out 'waterworks, jettes d'eau and a canal'.[4] Defoe described the Palace as 'the finest and largest new house built in Scotland'.

Royston also helped the Duchess in the pursuit of a long and acrimonious lawsuit with her younger son Henry, Earl of Deloraine. He had pursued a successful career in the army, rising to the rank of major general, and was given his earldom by Queen Anne in 1706, when he became a member of the last Scottish Parliament before the Act of Union, for which he voted. Following his brother's death Deloraine petitioned the Lords of Session claiming that, as the sole surviving son of the Duke of Monmouth, he had a right to the latter's estate, valued at £50,000, now that the forfeiture had been rescinded. His mother responded that the £50,000 had been a gift to her by King James II, that from it she had paid a number of Monmouth's debts and in 1688 had given Deloraine ('who was then destitute of any means of provision' – he was only twelve years old) £20,000. The case dragged on until

4
These plans do not seem to have been carried out.

1724, when the Lords of Session finally rejected Deloraine's claim, and it caused the Duchess much anguish, 'It is a melancholy victory against a son, yet the world will see I have not been a wicked parent', she wrote to Royston. She never forgave her younger son, and in her will she reproached him with gracelessness and extravagance; she left him only £5, with the rest of her estate going to her grandson Francis. 'Harry would be Duke of Buccleuch if Francis had not heirs male – God bless Francis and give him sons and no daughters'. In the event Deloraine died suddenly in 1730, two years before his mother. The Duchess died in London in 1732 at the age of eighty-one, having outlived all her children and even the first wife of her grandson Francis. Having often spoken of her wish to return to Scotland, she was buried at her own request in the family vault at Dalkeith.

CHAPTER SEVEN

Duke Francis, Duke Henry and Duke Charles

Francis, 2nd Duke of Buccleuch

Francis, Duchess Anna's eldest grandson, was thirty-eight when he succeeded to the Dukedom. His grandmother had hoped to marry him to Lady Jane Douglas, sister of the Duke of Douglas, and had expressed her delight that 'my great project of having my grandson no stranger to his own country is in all likelihood not to be disappointed by marrying a Scots lady'; but the engagement was broken off, and instead he married in 1720 another Lady Jane Douglas, also a 'Scots lady', daughter of the second Duke of Queensberry. Duke Francis was made a Knight of the Thistle in 1725 and was elected a representative peer in the Westminster Parliament in 1734. Although based in the south he paid frequent visits to Dalkeith and took a close interest in its development, and in particular that of East Park, which he seems to have preferred to the Palace itself: he regularly spent the night at East Park after having dined at Dalkeith. From his home at Hall Place, Berkshire, he sent a stream of letters (signed 'Your humble servant, Buccleuch') to his chamberlain Gilbert Grierson at Dalkeith about the remodelling and furnishing of East Park, and arranged for a large number of trees to be shipped to the estate. Some of these were used to form a new avenue from the Palace to East Park, with a new bridge known as the Laundry Bridge to carry it across the South Esk; and the rest were planted to create a Wilderness, a geometrical pattern of trees divided by grass walks, between the main avenue to the Palace and the South Esk, replacing the garden planted by Duchess Anna. In 1727 William Adam was commissioned to develop steep banks on the north, west and south sides of the Palace, supported by a timber frame on the west side above the North Esk. In 1740 a major addition to the estate was built in the form of an elegant stable block for sixty horses and staff, designed by William Adam, beyond the Wilderness, with a new kitchen garden next to it. The old stables in front of the Palace were demolished, and statues were erected in the Wilderness and in the East Park garden.

The first Royal visitor to the Palace since Charles I arrived, uninvited, in 1745. The Young Pretender, Prince Charles Edward ('Bonnie Prince Charlie'), approached Edinburgh with a substantial Jacobite army, and Duke Francis called out his tenants at Dalkeith to join the citizens of Edinburgh in defending the capital; but his efforts were feebly supported and resistance to the Jacobites soon melted away. Prince Charles Edward entered the city on 17th September, took up residence at the Palace of Holyroodhouse, and had his father, the Old Pretender (son of King James II) proclaimed King. Having defeated the Government

7.1 The Stable block.

7.2 Portrait of Prince Charles Edward Stewart.

forces under General Cope at the battle of Prestonpans on 21st September he held court at Holyroodhouse until the end of October, when his Grand Council after much debate decided to march on England. By this time the Jacobite army had swelled to some 5,500 men, and on 31st October they marched from Edinburgh and set up an encampment on the banks of the North Esk on the Dalkeith estate. The plan was to divide into two columns to march by different routes to the border at Carlisle. The Prince left Holyroodhouse the same day, and after spending the night at Pinkie House in Musselburgh set up his headquarters in Dalkeith Palace on 1st

November. Duke Francis was not in residence and the Prince and his staff seem to have made free with his reluctant hospitality: we are told that the Prince dined on chicken, duck, oysters and brandy. He stayed at the Palace for two nights, and on 3rd November he and his army marched south.

Duke Francis's first wife had died of smallpox in 1729, leaving him with two sons and three daughters. In 1744 he married again (his new wife, Alice Powell, was said to be a Windsor washerwoman) and he continued to live at Hall Place, with regular visits to Dalkeith until his death in 1751. Both his sons had died before him: the elder son, Francis Earl of Dalkeith, had married in 1742 Lady Caroline Campbell, daughter of the Duke of Argyll, through whom he inherited Caroline House on the Granton estate in north-west Edinburgh.[1] Earl Francis bought Bowhill in the Ettrick valley (now the principal seat of the Dukes of Buccleuch) for his younger brother Charles, so that he could stand for the Selkirkshire seat in Parliament; but Charles died the following year while still an undergraduate at Oxford. Earl Francis himself died of smallpox at Adderbury in Oxfordshire in 1750, a year before his father, and both father and son were buried in the family vault at Dalkeith.

Henry, 3rd Duke of Buccleuch

It was thus Duke Francis's eldest surviving grandson Henry who succeeded as third Duke of Buccleuch at the age of five. His mother remarried in 1755 the Hon. Charles Townshend, who was to pursue a distinguished political career culminating in his appointment as Chancellor of the Exchequer in Lord Chatham's administration in 1767.[2] Townshend took a close interest in the education of his stepchildren; Duke Henry was sent to Eton in 1757, and it was Townshend who suggested that after Eton he

1
Coincidentally Caroline House had previously been called Royston House, and had belonged to Duchess Anna's adviser Lord Royston; he sold it to the Duke of Argyll, who renamed it after his daughter.

2
Townshend is chiefly remembered for having introduced to the American colonies the tax on tea which provoked the Boston Tea Party.

7.3 Henry, 3rd Duke of Buccleuch.

should go on a tour of Europe. On a visit to Glasgow Townshend had met Adam Smith, then Professor of Moral Philosophy at Glasgow University, and he now asked Smith to accompany the young Duke as his tutor. David Hume, the philosopher, who had introduced Adam Smith to Townshend, tried to persuade him to send the young Duke to study under Smith at Glasgow University instead of sending them abroad; but Smith was happy to accept Townshend's offer of a life annuity of £300 a year, and was attracted by the opportunity to meet some of the distinguished European philosophers and economists with whose works he was already familiar.

7.4 Adam Smith.

So at the beginning of 1764 Adam Smith left his post in Glasgow and set off with Duke Henry for Europe; they were joined a few months later by the Duke's brother Campbell. Unlike most young aristocrats of the time (such as Henry's future brother-in-law the Marquis of Monthermer, son of the Duke of Montagu), Henry and Campbell did not embark on the conventional Grand Tour, which focussed on Italy and the acquisition of works of art: apart from a couple of months in Geneva they spent the whole two and a half years in France. Adam Smith clearly took his duties as a tutor seriously: after staying briefly in Paris with David Hume who was in the British Embassy there, they travelled to Toulouse, home of France's second oldest university and spent no less than eighteen months there.[3]

3
Smith wrote to David Hume that he was finding Toulouse rather boring, and that he had 'begun to write a book to pass away the time' – the origin of 'The Wealth of Nations'.

From there they went to Geneva, where Smith met Voltaire. In December 1765 they returned to Paris: David Hume had met a wide circle of French philosophers and economists while he was there from 1763 to 1765, and Adam Smith was welcomed at the various *salons* where they met. This experience was no doubt shared by the young Duke and his brother, and there can have been few young men of their time who were better educated.

In August 1766 Duke Henry visited the camp of the French army at Compiegne as a guest of King Louis XV, and there he caught a fever and was confined to bed for several weeks; Adam Smith sat day after day at his bedside and sent frequent bulletins to Townshend. The Duke was eventually restored to health and they returned to Paris; but in October Henry's brother Campbell also succumbed to a fever, and Smith had to write to Lady Frances Scott, sister of the two young men, to break the news that Campbell had died.[4] This cut short the Duke's visit to Europe, and at the beginning of November he and Adam Smith returned home, with Campbell's body which was buried at Dalkeith.

Duke Henry and his tutor spent the winter

7.5 Duke Henry with his family, with the Montagu Bridge in the background. The man on the extreme right is Charles, who became the 4th Duke.

of 1766–67 in London, where Townshend was now Chancellor of the Exchequer and evidently hoped to prepare his stepson for a career in politics.[5] In May 1767 Duke Henry married Lady Elizabeth Montagu, daughter of the Earl of Cardigan who later became 3rd Duke of Montagu, and on the eve of his twenty-first birthday he and his bride took up residence at Dalkeith Palace. The celebration of his coming of age had to be postponed because of Townshend's death. Encouraged by Adam Smith (who stayed with him at Dalkeith for two months) he then decided to settle down among his tenants and look after his estates – the first member of his family to live permanently in Scotland since the second Earl of Buccleuch. Adam Smith returned to his native Kirkcaldy, but remained in close contact throughout the rest of his life with the Duke, who clearly held him in great affection and who in 1777 secured for him a post as Commissioner of Customs in Edinburgh.

Duke Henry and his beautiful Duchess made themselves extremely popular both with their tenants and with the people of Scotland at large. In 1770 the Duchess's brother, the Marquis of Monthermer, died, and when their father died in 1790 she inherited the Montagu estates including Boughton House in Northamptonshire, which is now one of the principal Buccleuch residences; then in 1810, when the fourth Duke of Queensberry died without heirs,

4
There was later a rumour that Campbell had been murdered in a Paris street.

5
When Townshend died the Duke is recorded as saying that while he regretted his stepfather's death he had the consolation that it left him at liberty of choosing his own life, for if Townshend had survived he might have been 'drawn into the vortex of politics much against his will'.

Duke Henry became through his grandmother the fifth Duke of Queensberry, again with large estates including Drumlanrig Castle in Dumfriesshire.[6] The Duke was now by far the biggest landowner in Scotland. He and the Duchess had seven children, three sons (of whom the eldest died in infancy) and four daughters. The elder surviving son Charles became the fourth Duke, and the younger, Henry, succeeded through his mother to the title of Lord Montagu of Boughton. There is a charming portrait of the family at Bowhill.

Duke Henry continued the development

7.6 The interior corridor of the Ice House, with stairs leading up to ground level.

of the Dalkeith estate. In 1768 an ice house, which still stands, was constructed to the south-west of the Palace; it is enormous, with an ice chamber ten metres deep approached through a ten-metre passage with four doors at right-angle bends and a surrounding passage with hooks for the hanging of game. The following year the formal courtyard in front of the Palace was replaced with an oval lawn. In 1773 Duke Henry extended the estate by buying the property of Castlesteads across the river from East Park, and in the 1770s a menagerie was established at East Park, with a bear, tiger cats, owls, storks and racoons.[7]

In 1769 Duke Henry commissioned an artist named George Barret to paint a series of views of the Palace and the park; these now hang at Bowhill, and give a vivid impression of what the estate looked like in the early part of Duke Henry's time. In 1776 James Craig, the designer of Edinburgh's New Town, produced a plan for remodelling the Palace, adding wings to it, but the Duke rejected these. Later he engaged James Playfair to design new gates, known as the 'Duke's Gates' (1784), at the east end of Dalkeith High Street 'to form an imposing definition of the separateness of estate and town'; Playfair also designed a new bow window for the Library (1786) in the centre of the seventeenth-century north side of the Palace. In 1792 a handsome new bridge, the Montagu Bridge,

6

The Scottish dukedom of Queensberry, unlike the English dukedom of Montagu, could pass through the female line; the Duke of Buccleuch therefore became also Duke of Queensberry, and the family name became Montagu Douglas Scott.

7

Monkeys and canaries were kept at Castlesteads, and the whole menagerie was moved there in 1800 after many of the animals had died. In 1827 a pair of emus joined the menagerie: they had been given to Sir Walter Scott by an ex-convict named George Harper who had been deported to New South Wales but who, thanks to an intervention by Sir Walter with the Governor, had become a prosperous farmer. Sir Walter agreed to accept the emus thinking that they were the same size as parrots, but when they arrived standing six feet tall he appealed to Duke Henry's grandson, Duke Walter Francis, to give them sanctuary at Dalkeith.

7.7 Robert Adam's design for the Montagu Bridge. The images of stags on the parapet frightened the horses, and were removed.

7.8 Montagu Bridge as it is now.

was built across the North Esk to a design by Robert Adam (completed after his death by his brother James). The bridge was commissioned by Duke Henry to mark the union between the Scott and Montagu families, and is one of the most elegant constructions on the estate: it is a single semicircular arch of sandstone between tall parapets, and there is an excellent view of it from Playfair's bow window in the Library of the Palace.

While adhering to his resolve not to get involved in politics, the Duke also took a lively interest in the public affairs of Scotland. His first venture was a disaster: in 1769 he was persuaded by his great-uncle, the third Duke of Queensberry, to join him in setting up a new bank designed to stimulate the Scottish economy. The business of the bank, officially called Douglas, Heron and Company but usually known as the 'Ayr Bank', was secured not by gold or other realisable assets but by land. At first it prospered, with a large number of Lowland gentry investing their savings in it; but after less than three years the bank crashed with liabilities of more than a million pounds against nominal capital of £150,000. The Bank of England sued the two founding Dukes for twice that amount, but the Lord Advocate, Sir James Montgomery, steered through Parliament the Bank of Ayr Act which created financial instruments through which the Dukes could meet their

debts. Some of the claims against them continued for sixty years, but because of the immense wealth of the Buccleuch and Queensberry estates they survived the loss.

Other ventures were more successful. Duke Henry formed an alliance with Henry Dundas, the future Viscount Melville, who owned the neighbouring estate of Melville Castle and who was on his way to becoming the most powerful man in Scotland; with Dundas he helped to finance the construction of the Forth-Clyde Canal; and he assisted Dundas in undermining the position of the latter's distant kinsman and political rival, Sir Lawrence Dundas. In 1777 the Duke replaced Sir Lawrence as Governor of the Royal Bank of Scotland. He controlled a number of parliamentary constituencies through the system of 'faggot votes', whereby a landlord could give his tenants the property rights qualifying them to vote in parliamentary elections provided they voted in accordance with the landlord's wishes. He used his influence to help Dundas to dominate Scottish politics, and to support the administration of the younger Pitt. When France declared war on Britain in 1778, he raised a regiment of 'fencibles' (a volunteer militia for home defence) and took the rank of colonel. The regiment was involved in restoring order in Edinburgh after anti-popery riots the following year, but was disbanded when the war ended. When war broke out again in

1793 he advised Pitt and Dundas on the creation of a Scottish militia, and in 1803 he became colonel of two of its regiments.

In 1796 the exiled Comte d'Artois, youngest brother of Louis XVI of France, took up residence at Holyrood. Duke Henry and his elder son, the Earl of Dalkeith, were present at his first levee on 8th January. Thereafter the Comte and his family were frequent visitors to Dalkeith Palace until he left in 1803. A particularly close friendship developed between the Duchess and the Duc d'Angouleme, son of the Comte, who wrote to her frequently after his departure from Edinburgh in 1799. The Comte d'Artois was reported as saying, after calling on the Duchess at Dalkeith, that he felt as if she were a mighty sovereign and he an insignificant foreigner. In due course he succeeded his brother Louis XVIII as King Charles X in 1824.

Duke Henry was the first President of the Royal Society of Edinburgh, and with his wife he founded the Royal Blind Asylum in Edinburgh. He was Lord Lieutenant of Midlothian, East Lothian and Roxburgh, and was the first member of his family to be Captain-General of the Royal Company of Archers (the Sovereign's bodyguard in Scotland), a post which has been held by nearly all his successors including the present Duke. His service to his country was recognised by the award of the Order of the Thistle in 1767 and the Order of the Garter in 1794. He died at Dalkeith Palace in 1812, and was buried in the family chapel.

Charles, 4th Duke of Buccleuch

He was succeeded by his elder surviving son Charles (1772–1819). Like his father he had been educated at Eton, but then went on to Christ Church, Oxford, where he became a Doctor of Civil Law at the age of twenty-one. As Earl of Dalkeith, he was elected to Parliament in the same year and remained an MP for various English constituencies until 1807. He gave his enthusiastic support to the government of Pitt the Younger, but spoke rarely in the House. In 1795 he married his second cousin Harriet Townshend, daughter of Viscount Sydney, and they had seven children. He was a keen amateur cricketer, a member of the MCC, and in 1797 he played in four first-class matches, including two at Lord's. In the same year he and his brother Henry were among the founding members of the Edinburgh Light Dragoons, a volunteer cavalry regiment formed under the perceived threat of a French invasion. Another member was the future Sir Walter Scott, and this was the beginning of a lifelong friendship. Scott was thereafter a frequent visitor to Dalkeith Palace, and his first major poem, 'The Lay of the Last Minstrel', was written at the request

7.9 Charles, 4th Duke of Buccleuch known as 'the Pink Boy' by Sir Joshua Reynolds.

of Lady Dalkeith and dedicated to her husband. At the latter's prompting, Duke Henry persuaded Dundas (who by this time controlled all patronage in Scotland) to appoint Scott as Sheriff of Selkirkshire, and later as a Clerk of the Court of Session. Lord Dalkeith was Lord Lieutenant of Selkirkshire and later of Dumfriesshire and Midlothian, and succeeded his father as Captain-General of the Royal Company of Archers. He was made a Knight of the Thistle on acceding to the Dukedom in 1812.

Duke Charles at once set about rebuilding

7.10 Raeburn's portrait of Sir Walter Scott.

Bowhill, the family seat near Selkirk, as a retreat from the formal life at Dalkeith where he could enjoy the country pleasures of hunting, fishing and shooting. In 1815, when the refurbishment was complete, he held a convivial dinner party at Bowhill which included his sister Elizabeth and her husband, the 10th Earl of Home, and Sir Walter Scott and his friend James Hogg, the 'Ettrick Shepherd', to whom the Duke had given the life rent of a farm in the Yarrow valley. At this dinner it was agreed to arrange a football match between the shepherds of Ettrick and Yarrow (mostly Duke Charles's tenants and including James Hogg), captained by the Earl of Home, and a team from the neighbouring towns of Selkirk, Hawick and Galashiels. The result was the famous 'Carterhaugh Ba' Game', played on a meadow near Bowhill at the meeting of the Ettrick and Yarrow rivers. There were several hundred players on each side, and the game lasted for five hours. The rules did not forbid handling of the ball, and it can be argued that this was the first game of Rugby Football, some eight years before William Webb Ellis picked up the ball at Rugby School. At half time the team from the border towns was winning, and Sir Walter Scott persuaded the men of Galashiels to defect to the side of Buccleuch's shepherds, who then won the second half. Walter Scott wrote a song to commemorate the occasion, and the Carter-

haugh Ba' Game has been re-enacted from time to time ever since.

Sadly Duke Charles had only seven years to enjoy the dukedom: in 1819 he fell ill with tuberculosis and went for his health to Lisbon, where he died at the age of 47.

CHAPTER EIGHT

Duke Walter Francis

It is a melancholy fact that until the twentieth century only one firstborn Buccleuch son, the sixth Duke, survived to succeed to the title. Duke Charles's eldest son, like his elder brother, died in childhood (of measles at the age of ten), and it was his second son, Walter Francis, who now succeeded to the title as fifth Duke at the age of thirteen. His uncle, Lord Montagu of Boughton, and Sir Walter Scott were appointed as his guardians (another mark of the close friendship between Sir Walter and Duke Charles). He was educated at Eton, and spent some of his school holidays staying with Lord Montagu at his estate of Ditton Park near the school.

Sir Walter Scott was largely instrumental in persuading King George IV to pay a visit to Scotland in 1822. The King when he was Prince Regent had enjoyed Sir Walter's novels, with their romantic depiction of Scottish history, and had invited Sir Walter to dine with him at Carlton House. Scott pointed out to the King that he (the King) was a direct descendant of the Stuart Kings of Scotland, and reminded him that no British sovereign had visited the northern kingdom since King Charles II in 1650. Doubts were expressed about where the King might stay if he went to Scotland, since the Palace of Holyroodhouse was in a state of dilapidation. It was probably through Sir Walter that Lord Montagu learned of these doubts, so he wrote to the Home Secretary, Robert Peel, offering Dalkeith Palace as a

8.1 Sir David Wilkie's portrait of King George IV, which the King presented to his host, the 5th Duke of Buccleuch.

home for the King in Scotland. This offer was gratefully accepted, and as a result Duke Walter Francis found himself, at the age of sixteen, playing host to the King and his entourage at Dalkeith.

There were only two months between the announcement of the King's visit in June 1822 and his arrival in August, and this time was taken up with frantic preparations both at Holyrood, where the reception rooms were refurbished, and at Dalkeith, where a new bed was acquired for the King (now at Bowhill) and the suite of rooms on the first floor on the west side of the palace were smartened up

8.2 Walter Francis, 5th Duke of Buccleuch.

for the King's use. A new avenue was laid across the Montagu Bridge to the Edinburgh road, with new gates forming a ceremonial entrance to the estate, and a triumphal arch was erected over the gates leading from the town to the estate. A new dairy was established by the King's purveyor, Mr Florance, to provide butter and cream for the King, with the milk and buttermilk being distributed to the poor. A 'Poor's Pot' was also established where the poor of Dalkeith were served with 'good wholesome broth and broken victuals', and lamps were erected every forty yards along the road leading from Edinburgh to the new gates. When all was ready the arrangements were inspected by Lord Montagu and the Marquis of Lothian (who was Lord Lieutenant) and they pronounced themselves satisfied.

The King's visit aroused great enthusiasm throughout Scotland, and when it became known that the visit would be confined to Edinburgh some 50,000 people from all over the country descended on the capital. Many of them, encouraged by Sir Walter, wore highland dress which until forty years earlier had been banned following the 1745 rebellion, but which was now back in fashion. Although south of the border the King had until recently been highly unpopular (and the subject of a series of scurrilous cartoons) his visit to Ireland the previous year had gone well, and thanks in large measure to careful preparation by Sir Walter his Scottish subjects entered into the spirit of the occasion and gave him a warm welcome. He was greeted by cheering crowds wherever he went, and the public occasions of the visit – a Levee and Drawing Room[1] at Holyrood, a cavalry review on Portobello Sands, a civic banquet in Parliament Hall, a church service in St Giles Cathedral, two balls at the Assembly Rooms and a performance of 'Rob Roy' at the theatre – were attended by nearly all the great and good of Scotland. The visit lasted from 15th to 29th August, and the King stayed at Dalkeith Palace throughout.

On the eve of the King's arrival Lord and Lady Montagu and their nieces and nephews (including Duke Walter Francis) moved from Dalkeith to a hotel in Edinburgh, taking with them a few personal servants and leaving the majority of the household staff, under the command of the Duke's Chamberlain and Housekeeper, at the King's disposal. Lord Montagu and the Duke were invited to dine in a small party at Dalkeith on the second day of the visit, when the King had stayed on the estate all day and, in the words of Robert Mudie, a contemporary chronicler, 'resigned himself to the simple pleasures of rural retirement'. The following day (17th August) there was a Levee at Holyrood, for which the King arrayed himself in full highland dress, saying as he emerged from his dressing room at Dalkeith 'I cannot help smiling at myself'. The fact that the kilt emphasised his *embon-point* and that he wore flesh-coloured tights beneath his kilt to conceal his gouty legs led to a number of other discreet smiles among the company who saw him, though Robert Mudie loyally recorded that the costume 'displayed his manly and graceful figure to great advantage'. Sir David Wilkie's painting of the King in his kilt is in the Royal Collection, but a miniature version of it was presented to the Duke and is now at Bowhill.

After another day of rest at Dalkeith on 18th August the King went to Holyrood on two successive days, for audiences on the first

1
A levee was attended by men only, a Drawing Room was primarily intended for ladies to be presented to the Sovereign.

day and a Drawing Room for five hundred ladies on the second; on these occasions, and for the rest of the visit, he reverted to Field Marshal's uniform. On 21st August, after another day within the walls of Dalkeith, he gave a large dinner party at which music was played by a band led by the celebrated violinist Nathaniel Gow (son of the even better known Neil Gow), who had often been invited to private parties given by the King when Prince Regent. Duke Walter Francis was seated on the King's right, treated by him with great amiability, and sent from time to time to tell the band what music the King wanted played. When the Duke hesitated, the King slapped him on the shoulder and said 'Come, Buccleuch, you are the youngest man in the company and must make yourself useful'. When the servants offered the Duke a glass of liqueur the King said 'No, no! it is too strong for His Grace to drink'.

On 22nd August the King spent the morning riding in the grounds of Dalkeith on a large white horse which he had bought just before leaving London; he was apparently obliged to use a ladder to mount it. It was raining, but he was determined to get used to the horse before appearing on it the following day at the cavalry review at Portobello, where the ever-tactful Robert Mudie described him as mounting and dismounting 'with great ease, agility and neatness'. In the evening the Duke dined with him again, but is not recorded as having taken any further part in the programme apart from attending the church service at St Giles on 25th August, at the end of which the King shook his hand. Among the numerous toasts drunk at the banquet given by the Lord Provost in Parliament Hall on 24th August was one by Lord Strathmore to 'the King's young landlord, the Duke of Buccleuch' but the reply was given by Lord Montagu. The King paid private visits to Lord Melville at Melville Castle on the 27th and to the Marquis of Lothian at Newbattle Abbey on the 28th. He left Dalkeith on the morning of 29th August, and after lunch at Hopetoun House in West Lothian with the Earl of Hopetoun embarked on the yacht *Royal George* to return to London.

The young Duke returned to the Palace with his uncle, aunt and siblings, and in due course went back to school. From Eton he had intended to follow in his father's footsteps by going to Christ Church, Oxford; but the Dons refused to accommodate his stud of six hunters, so he went instead to St John's College, Cambridge, where he graduated with an MA in 1827. Two years later he married Charlotte Thynne, daughter of the Marquess of Bath, and they had four sons and three daughters. He was now owner of three large estates in Scotland – Dalkeith, Bowhill and Drumlanrig – as well as Boughton House in England.

8.3 William Burn's design for a new palace.

He devoted much of his time and energy for the rest of his long life – he was Duke for sixty-five years – to the development of his estates. At Dalkeith he replaced the formal 'wilderness' with plain woodland, and established a bowling green where the orchard had been on the low-lying ground near the Montagu Bridge. From 1831 onwards William Burn, one of the leading Scottish architects of the day, carried out a number of projects for the Duke. He blocked up the main entrance of the Palace in the centre of the east façade (George IV having complained of drafts during his visit) and constructed a new entrance porch in the south-east corner of the courtyard.[2] Burn also produced a design for a new Palace in sumptuous Jacobean style which was (fortunately) rejected, but a model of which remains on display at Bowhill. He designed the splendid twelve-sided Conservatory (1834), in the same Jacobean style, which was intended as the centrepiece of a new formal garden designed by W.S. Gilpin to the north of the stable block. This garden was never completed, but the Conservatory still stands.[3] Burn also constructed a new service wing on the south side of the palace, and he and his partner David Bryce built in 1843 the episcopal church of St Mary just inside the town gate of the Palace which served as the palace chapel for many years. It has an impressive interior, with a steep hammerbeam roof, a stone pulpit, Minton tiles, and one of the only two hydraulically

2
Burn's entrance porch is still there, but the main entrance was restored in 1973.

3
The Conservatory was described as 'the most elaborate and probably the best specimen of a truly architectural conservatory in the kingdom'; but the site on low ground near the South Esk was unhappily chosen, the water supply was inadequate, the boilers in the basement smoked, and the running costs were very high; and it soon fell out of use.

8.4 The Conservatory.

8.5 The King's Gates

blown organs in Scotland. Burn and Bryce were also responsible for building a new King's Gate and Lodge on the Edinburgh Road, replacing the gates erected for the King's visit, with elaborate wrought-iron gates from Holland House in London.

In 1838 the Duke appointed a new Head Gardener, Charles McIntosh, who was the foremost horticulturalist of his day and author of several successful gardening books.[4] McIntosh submitted plans for a new walled garden on the south-facing slope across the North Esk from the Palace, and these were approved by the Duke. The garden covered twenty acres, and was at the time the second largest in the country after the royal gardens at Windsor. It had an impressive array of greenhouses, a tropical plant house, vineries, and separate houses for peaches, camellias, orchids, figs and other fruits; and the Gardener's House was described by McIntosh as 'one of the best and most commodious in the kingdom, and quite in accordance with the liberality of His Grace, who provides every member of his various extensive establishments with houses not merely comfortable, but in fact superior to those of servants in general'. The gardens became famous throughout Britain, and were the subject of numerous articles in horticultural journals. The land was sold off to developers in the 1970s, and though part of the walls survive at the Lugton end of the estate the area is now a housing estate.

Duke Walter Francis was active in developing his other estates as well as Dalkeith (though he does not seem to have paid much attention to Boughton, where there was little development until the beginning of the twentieth century). At Drumlanrig the woodlands had been devastated and the farmland neglected during the time of the notorious fourth Duke of Queensberry, known as 'Old Q', who lived a dissolute life in London at the expense of his estates and died at the age of eighty-one in 1810. Duke Walter Francis embarked on an ambitious programme to restore the woodlands and modernise the farmland, and laid the foundations of what is now a prosperous estate. He also employed William Burn to rebuild the family home in London, Montagu House on the north bank of the Thames, in a flamboyant French renaissance style.[5] But it was at Granton on the coast of the Firth of Forth that the Duke

4
McIntosh had previously been gardener to Prince Leopold of Saxe-Coburg, widower of King George IV's daughter Princess Caroline, and from 1830 King Leopold I of the Belgians. He had been in charge of the gardens both at Claremont, Prince Leopold's house in Surrey, and at the royal palace of Laeken near Brussels.

5
Montagu House was used increasingly by the family until it was requisitioned by the Government during the First World War, and subsequently demolished to make room for the present Ministry of Defence building.

left his most significant mark. His grandfather, Duke Henry, had inherited through his mother the Caroline Park estate at Granton on the coast of the Firth of Forth, north-west of Edinburgh, and between 1835 and 1863 Duke Walter Francis, with technical advice from Robert Stephenson the lighthouse builder, built a new deep-water harbour there with a pier and two breakwaters, using stone from Granton Quarry which was also on the estate.[6] The Duke also built a new harbour at Burntisland on the north coast of the Forth and established between the two harbours the first roll-on-roll-off train ferry in the world, which operated until the building of the Forth Bridge in 1890.

It was at Granton Pier that Queen Victoria and Prince Albert first set foot in Scotland in 1842 – much to the chagrin of the magistrates of Leith, who appealed both to the Queen and to the Duke of Buccleuch (as Lord Lieutenant of Midlothian) for the Port of Leith to be chosen, as the traditional port for Edinburgh. But Leith was not as well developed as it became later, and the Royal Yacht, the *Royal George*, could moor alongside the pier at Granton whereas George IV, when he arrived at Leith, had had to go ashore by barge. There had been an outbreak of scarlet fever among the residents of Holyrood, and although a great deal of refurbishment had been carried out since George IV's visit it was thought unsafe for the Queen to stay there, so like George IV she stayed at Dalkeith Palace instead.

Queen Victoria's visit began in a certain amount of chaos. The *Royal George* was delayed by bad weather, and although the visit was supposed to begin on 31st August it was not until after midnight the Royal Yacht reached Granton. The crowds which had gathered to greet the Queen had to wait until the following morning; and the Lord Provost and Council, together with the Royal Company of Archers, who had been on the alert the day before, were caught unawares when the Queen stepped ashore at nine o'clock on 1st September, an hour earlier than had been planned. Due to some failure of communication the guns of Edinburgh Castle did not fire their salute until the royal procession was well on its way to the city, and a good deal of confusion resulted. However, the Queen was warmly welcomed, and both she and Prince Albert were delighted with the city. 'It is quite beautiful', wrote the Queen in her diary, 'totally unlike anything else I have seen; and what is even more, Albert, who has seen so much, says it is unlike anything *he* ever saw'. They drove through the city and then on to Dalkeith, where the Duchess of Buccleuch conducted them to their rooms on the first floor, which the Queen found very comfortable. Next morning, after a breakfast of porridge and 'Finnan Haddies', the royal party walked in the grounds of the Palace,

6
Stone from the Granton Quarry was also used, after a nationwide competition, for Nelson's column in Trafalgar Square.

which the Queen described as 'very beautiful, wild and hilly', and in the afternoon they drove through cheering crowds in Dalkeith and Lasswade and in a thick Scotch mist, to Melville Castle. The Duchess of Buccleuch (who was the Queen's Mistress of the Robes) drove with the Queen, with the Duke on horseback behind.

On 3rd September the Queen and Prince Albert drove into Edinburgh to see the sights, including the Palace of Holyroodhouse (from a safe distance), the Royal Mile, and the Castle, where they walked to the top and admired the view; and Prince Albert and Duke Walter Francis climbed to the top of Arthur's Seat.

8.6 The arrival of Queen Victoria and Prince Albert at Dalkeith Palace.

They drove out to Dalmeny, Lord Rosebery's estate to the west of the city, and then along the shore to Leith before returning to Dalkeith. Next day, Sunday, they attended a service in Dalkeith Palace (there was some press criticism of the fact that they did not worship in public at St Giles Cathedral) and later visited the Marquis of Lothian at Newbattle Abbey and the Earl of Dalhousie at Dalhousie Castle. On 5th September the Queen held a formal Drawing Room in the first-floor Gallery at Dalkeith – the only occasion on which a Royal Drawing Room has been held in a private house. The royal party left Dalkeith on the morning of the 6th and, having crossed the Forth at Queensferry, spent a week in the Highlands, staying at Scone Palace, Taymouth Castle and Drummond Castle. The Queen's journal is full of enthusiasm for all that they saw, and Prince Albert had his first experience of deer-stalking. The Duke and Duchess of Buccleuch went with them, and at the end of their tour they returned for two nights to Dalkeith Palace before returning to London.[7]

By the time of Queen Victoria's visit Duke Walter Francis had become a member of Sir Robert Peel's first Conservative Government: he was appointed Lord Privy Seal in February 1842. He was a strong supporter of Peel, but when the latter decided in 1845 to repeal the protectionist Corn Laws – a decision which split the Tory party – the Duke of Buccleuch,

7
Queen Victoria visited Dalkeith Palace again in1872 with two of her children, Princess Beatrice and Prince Leopold. She stopped there in the course of a drive from Holyrood, because she wanted to show the children the rooms in which she and Prince Albert had stayed in 1842. Two years later the Princess of Wales (the future Queen Alexandra) paid her first visit accompanied by her father, King Christian IX of Denmark, and her brother Prince Valdemar.

as a major landowner, was one of the two members of the Cabinet who opposed the measure. The other, Lord Stanley, eventually resigned over the issue, but Peel appealed to the Duke's loyalty and he agreed not to oppose the repeal.[8] He was rewarded by being promoted to Lord President of the Council, but when Peel's government fell in July 1846 he was out of office, and his political career was virtually at an end. For the rest of his life he devoted himself to improving his estates and pursuing his interests as President of the Highland Agricultural Society, of the Society of Antiquaries, and of the British Association for the Advancement of Science, and as Chancellor of Glasgow University. He enriched the contents of his houses by acquiring some important 18th century French furniture and a large collection of Vincennes and Sevres porcelain, including over one hundred pieces from King Louis XV's own dining set. He was, as Charles McIntosh recorded, a generous employer and was popular with the citizens of Dalkeith; he supported the local sports clubs, opened the grounds of the Palace to the public twice a week, and gave a series of sumptuous balls, some of them with fireworks displays at the Palace to which local residents were invited. He died at Bowhill in 1884 at the age of seventy-seven and was buried in St Mary's Church in the grounds of Dalkeith Palace, which he had had built in1843 and which now holds a marble monument to him. The statue of Duke Walter Francis in West Parliament Square in Edinburgh, erected soon after his death 'by his fellow countrymen at home and abroad' is a fitting tribute to the affection and respect with which he was regarded.

8
Like his grandfather Duke Henry, Duke Walter Francis controlled a number of Parliamentary constituencies through the system of 'faggot votes'. When Peel threatened to resign because of the divisions in his Cabinet he told Prince Albert that 'Buccleuch would carry half Scotland with him'.

CHAPTER NINE

Duke William

Duke Walter Francis was succeeded by his eldest son William, who had been born in 1831 at Montagu House, Whitehall, the London residence of the family, and educated at Eton and Christ Church, Oxford. As Earl of Dalkeith he was elected as Conservative Member of Parliament for Midlothian in 1853, at the tender age of twenty-two; this was one of the last elections before the 1867 Electoral Reform Act which abolished 'faggot votes', the system by which successive Dukes of Buccleuch had been able to ensure that Conservative candidates were elected in constituencies where they held the majority of the land. William remained a Member of Parliament until 1868, when he was defeated in the election following the passage of the Reform Act. He was re-elected in 1874, but in that year the secret ballot was introduced which meant that tenants could vote against the wishes of their landlords without being found out. In the election of 1880 his opponent as Liberal candidate was none other than William Ewart Gladstone, who after conducting the celebrated 'Midlothian Campaign', defeated him by only 211 votes. The Earl of Dalkeith complained bitterly that many of those who had promised to vote for him had obviously failed to do so.[1] He was described by Lord Morley, in his life of Gladstone, as 'a Tory of the hardest and narrowest type'; but in his twenty-one years as an MP he appears only once in Hansard,

1 There is a persistent rumour among the townspeople of Dalkeith that the Duke was so incensed by their failure to re-elect his son that he decided to move out of Dalkeith Palace. In fact, however, it was only after the sixth Duke's death in 1914 that the family gave up living in the Palace (see Chapter Ten); and in the meantime the Duke showed every sign of benevolence towards the town.

9.1 William, 6th Duke of Buccleuch.

when he asked a question about a proposed Scottish Roads Bill in 1876.

In 1859 William married Lady Louisa Hamilton, daughter of the Duke of Abercorn, and they had six sons and two daughters. Soon after he succeeded to the Dukedom his eldest son Walter was tragically killed in a shooting accident in Achnacarry Forest in the Highlands and his second son John became Earl of Dalkeith (and eventually succeeded as seventh Duke). Duke William was a keen sportsman – an excellent shot and a member of the Royal Yacht Squadron – and a conscientious and considerate landlord of his huge estates.[2] Unlike his father, he played little part in public life; but he and his duchess (who was Mistress of the Robes to both Queen Victoria and Queen Alexandra) were prominent members of London society and entertained lavishly at Montagu House; and the Duke was host to a number of shooting parties at Bowhill and at Langholm Lodge (now demolished), one of the Buccleuch houses in Dumfriesshire. He also opened Dalkeith Palace to the public twice a week in summer, and in 1906 established ten acres of 'pleasure grounds' in the park to which members of the public were admitted when the family was not in residence.

At Dalkeith, the Duke and Duchess entertained King Edward VII as Prince of Wales in 1899, when he travelled between Edinburgh and Dalkeith by train and visited the Royal Highland Show; and in 1903, on his first visit to Scotland after his accession, he again stayed at Dalkeith with Queen Alexandra. This visit lasted for five days, and they carried

2
At his funeral it was said that he remembered the names and careers of even the humblest of his tenants, and took a constant interest in their welfare.

9.2 The Town Gates, decorated for the visit of King Edward VII.

out official engagements in Edinburgh on two days and in Glasgow on one day before returning direct from Dalkeith to London on a special train. In 1907 the Prince and Princess of Wales (the future King George V and Queen Mary) stayed at Dalkeith for a week, again arriving by train. They were the last members of the royal family to stay at the palace; but the fact that all these royal visitors preferred Dalkeith Palace to Holyrood (though they held receptions there) suggests that the royal apartments at Holyrood were less comfortable.

Certainly the various accounts which survive of the interior of Dalkeith Palace at this period give evidence of truly princely magnificence. A catalogue drawn up in 1890 listed more than four hundred paintings in the palace, including twelve portraits by Lely, six each by Van Dyck and Kneller, five by Reynolds and four by Gainsborough; twenty-seven paintings by Guardi and seven by Canaletto. In the Entrance Hall hung Wilkie's portrait of King George IV in Highland dress and nine other portraits; there was also a tapestry screen which is supposed to have been worked by Mary Queen of Scots. In the Marble Hall there still stands a full-size statue of the Duke of Wellington by Thomas Campbell, commissioned by the fifth Duke in 1828, and on the walls were two portraits and three scenes of battles in which the Duke of Monmouth had fought. On the marble

9.3 The Marble Hall, with the statue of the Duke of Wellington.

staircase above was the massive equestrian portrait of Monmouth which now hangs at Boughton House, together with no fewer than sixty-five other paintings and seven busts; the paintings were hung in tiers. On the staircase landing stood an exquisite Italian cabinet in ebony with silver-gilt plates, a wedding gift to Monmouth from his father Charles II.

The suite of State rooms on the west side, overlooking the North Esk, contained more of the Buccleuch treasures; in the Dining Room, which was hung with tapestry, was Kneller's portrait of Duchess Anna with her two sons; Holbein's portrait of Sir Nicholas Carew (now at Drumlanrig); Gainsborough's portraits of the Duke and Duchess of Montagu; Van Dyck's portrait of William and Mary of Orange; and the so-called "Dalkeith portrait" of Mary, Queen of Scots with a rose in her hand (the latter had been hung in East

9.4 The Dining Room.

Park in Duke Francis's day). In the Morning Room, which was hung with red damask, were the twenty-seven Guardis; and in the Book Room was a portrait of Mary of Modena (wife of James II) framed in marble and an ebony secretaire inlaid with silver.

The two rooms in the north-east corner of the ground floor remain very much as they were in the time of Duchess Anna: the

9.5 The Duchess's sitting room, with marble overmantel by Grinling Gibbons.

9.6 The Library.

Duchess's Closet has an unusual flower painting on a looking-glass, the work of a Hungarian artist names Jakob Bogdani who was fashionable at the Court of Queen Anne. He painted it for Duchess Anna's home at Moor Park, and she was so fond of it that she had it moved to Dalkeith when she began to rebuild the palace in the early 1700s. Next door, in the Duchess's Sitting Room, there is a marble fireplace with a beautifully carved marble overmantel depicting the story of Neptune and Galatea, the work of Grinling Gibbons, surmounted by a glass panel with Duchess Anna's monogram and coronet. This room had several pieces of Boulle period French furniture, and a balcony leading to an outside staircase. The Library, next in the enfilade of rooms on the north side, was formed in the 1780s by merging the Duke's Bedroom and Dressing Room, and it was here that Playfair constructed a bow window in 1786; the room contained Reynolds's

9.7 The first-floor Gallery, where Queen Victoria held a Drawing Room.

portrait of Duke Henry, flanked by charming portraits of his six children by Sir William Beechey. The Ante Library was hung with more paintings by Jan Wyck of scenes of battles in which the Duke of Monmouth distinguished himself in his youth.

The principal room on the first floor is the Gallery, which contained many of the finest paintings in the collection and some beautiful

9.8 The Canaletto Room.

French furniture, including two French cabinets which were given to Charles II by King Louis XIV of France, and which formed part of King Charles's wedding present to Monmouth. On the west side of the first floor was the Queen's Bedroom, where royal visitors from George IV to the future George V slept, with a Drawing Room next door hung with Canaletto paintings. Nearly all these works of art are now at Bowhill. Finally, in the Charter Room on the first floor (part of the old tower) were the Bellendain Banner[3] and the clothes worn by the Duke of Monmouth at his execution.

In 1909 the Duke and Duchess celebrated their Golden Wedding at the Palace, and with typical generosity Duke William marked the occasion by presenting a six-acre public park to the town of Dalkeith; he also gave the town a piece of land for the construction of a hospital.[4] In the same year the Duchess died, and was buried in the family vault in St Mary's Church in the grounds of the Palace where her father-in-law and her eldest son were also buried. Duke William himself was buried there when he died in 1914.

3
The Bellendaine Banner is the standard of the Buccleuch family; 'A Bellendaine' was the ancient war cry of the Scott family. Bellendaine, or Bellendean, is between Selkirk and Hawick in the Scottish Borders, not far from the farm of Buccleuch.

4
The Duke also made a substantial contribution to the cost of building the hospital, which was opened in 1912 and was known as the Dalkeith Fever Hospital. It is now a business centre.

CHAPTER TEN

The End of the Story

Duke William was the last member of the family to live at Dalkeith; indeed, he stayed at the Palace a great deal less often than his father had done. He gave up the post of Lieutenant Colonel of the Midlothian Yeomanry in 1872 and ceased to represent Midlothian in Parliament in 1880, and from then on his only official posts were as Justice of the Peace and Deputy Lieutenant of Selkirkshire and Deputy Lieutenant for Roxburghshire, for both of which Bowhill was a more convenient base. He spent the Christmas period and early spring regularly at Dalkeith, but for most of the rest of the year was at Bowhill, Drumlanrig or Langholm or at Montagu House in London – except of course when he entertained members of the Royal Family at Dalkeith. When the First World War broke out he was living at Montagu House, where he died towards the end of 1914. He was succeeded as seventh Duke by his son John, who had given up a career in the Royal Navy when his elder brother was killed, and who had been Member of Parliament for Roxburghshire from 1895 to 1906. Duke John was married in 1893 to the daughter of the Earl of Bradford, and they had eight children including the future Princess Alice, Duchess of Gloucester.[1]

The family stayed at Dalkeith for part of November and December 1914 for Duke William's funeral, but for the rest of the First

1
Princess Alice recorded in her memoirs that her father disliked pomp and protocol of all kinds. When invited to attend some function in the New Club in Princes Street in Edinburgh he agreed to do so only if the occasion was quite informal. As his car approached the Club he saw that the Lord Provost and Councillors of the city were assembled in full robes at the entrance waiting to receive him; so he instructed his chauffeur to stop at a tram stop, and emerged from the tram to greet them.

World War the Palace seems to have been unoccupied except for a few members of staff.

An army signalling school and the Midlothian Volunteer Regiment were based in the stables and the Conservatory, and dug trenches in the grounds; Duke John gave them permission to skate on the curling pond and to play baseball (oddly enough) on the cricket pitch. During the war Bowhill and Drumlanrig were used as hospitals, so the family spent Christmas and Easter at Boughton in Northamptonshire and the summer months at Langholm Lodge in Dumfriessshire, which had previously been used only for shooting parties. Montagu House was requisitioned for Government offices, and the family moved to a house in Grosvenor Place. When the war was over Duke John decided against moving back into Dalkeith House (as it was henceforth called). By this time the town of Dalkeith, which in the nineteenth century had been a flourishing market town with the largest grain market in Britain, had become an insalubrious coal mining and industrial town with a good deal of slum housing, which was not cleared until 1956. The Duke found that the beauty and tranquillity of the Ettrick valley (where Bowhill is situated) was greatly preferable. The furniture, paintings and other treasures from Dalkeith were gradually distributed among the other Buccleuch residences.[2] Dalkeith House was left as an empty shell; but when Duke John died in 1935 he was buried in St Mary's Church on the estate with his father and grandfather.

At the beginning of the Second World War the estate was again requisitioned, and part of the house was occupied by Polish troops of the 3rd Flanders Rifle Brigade, part of the 1st Polish Armoured Division; graffiti left by them are still visible on the wall of the third floor. The rest of the house was used for the storage of books, furniture and china which had not yet gone to other Buccleuch houses, and the Durham Light Infantry occupied part of the Park. After the war the north wing of the ground floor (where the private apartments of the Duke and Duchess had been) was used as offices of Buccleuch Estates Ltd.[3] There was a flat for the secretary of the company and his family, and a houseman and housekeeper each had a room on the first floor; the rest of the house remained empty. In 1932 the Stable Block was rented to the Greyhound Racing Association, who used it until 1989 as kennels for their dogs racing at Powderhall Stadium in Edinburgh.

In 1970 the eighth Duke rented the Palace to International Computers Limited, a large British company recently formed by the merger of several computer firms. They established a research and development centre in the Palace, and built in the grounds a computer house because computers needed air conditioning which could not be installed in

2
So were the contents of the wine cellars. In the course of clearing them eighteen bottles were found bearing the label 'General Monck's Amontillado'.

3
Buccleuch Estates Ltd. was founded in 1923 for the management of the Duke's estates, which include Bowhill in Selkirkshire, the Queensberry Estate (including Drumlanrig Castle) in Dumfries and Galloway, the Eskdale and Liddesdale Estate, and the Boughton Estate in Northamptonshire as well as Dalkeith Country Park.

the Palace itself. With the Duke's permission ICL carried out a substantial amount of renovation in the Palace, including the restoration in 1973 (by the architect W. Schomberg Scott) of the main central entrance which had been blocked up after the visit of George IV.

ICL ran into financial difficulties in the early 1980s (they were eventually absorbed by Fujitsu), and they moved out of the Palace in 1983. Then in 1986 the ninth Duke rented the Palace to a consortium of University of Wisconsin campuses, and it remains the headquarters of the University's 'Wisconsin in Scotland' programme under which students from Wisconsin live in the Palace and study a variety of subjects from their home campuses as well as Scottish history and culture. This programme, which gives most of the students a first experience of life beyond Wisconsin, is extremely popular.

The present (tenth) Duke of Buccleuch takes a close interest in Dalkeith Palace: he was married there in 1981, and in 1985 – when the house was empty between the occupation by ICL and the University of Wisconsin – he arranged a concert there of 18th and 19th century Scottish and European music, played by the Scottish Ensemble. In 2012, when the Duke relinquished the post of President of the National Trust for Scotland, he gave the traditional President's Ball in a marquee in front of the Palace. He has plans for the redevelopment of the Park, with a new Visitor Centre, restaurant and adventure playground

near the Stables and Conservatory. So although Dalkeith Palace is unlikely ever to be restored to its former glory, the grounds where King Charles I hunted and King George IV tried out his new horse will continue to give much pleasure to all who visit it.

10.1 The plan for the new Visitor Centre and Cafe behind the Stables.

Appendices

Appendix 1 Family Tree

The Grahams of Dalkeith

David I (1124–53)		**Sir William de Graham**
Malcolm IV (1153–65)		**Sir Peter de Graham**
		Sir Henry de Graham
William I (the Lion) (1165–1214)		
Alexander II (1214–49)		**Sir Henry de Graham**
Alexander III (1249–86)		**Sir Henry de Graham**
Margaret (1286–90)		
Interregnum (1290–2)		**Sir Nicholas de Graham**
John Balliol (1292–6)		
Interregnum (1296–1306)		**Sir John Graham**
Robert I (the Bruce) (1306–29)		
David II (1329–71)	**Sir John Graham**	**Margaret *m.* Sir William Douglas**

The Douglasses of Dalkeith

James Douglas of Lothian

Sir William Douglas (Knight of Liddesdale)
m. Margaret Graham

Sir John Douglas

King Robert III

Sir James Douglas *m.* Agnes Dunbar

Elizabeth *m.*

Sir James Douglas

King James II

Sir James Douglas

Henry Douglas of Borgue

Joanna *m.*

James, 1st Earl of Morton

King James IV

John, 2nd Earl of Morton

Katherine *m.*

James, 3rd Earl of Morton

Archibald, 5th Earl of Angus

George, Master of Angus

James, 3rd Earl of Morton

Archibald, 6th Earl of Angus

George Douglas of Pittendreich

David, 7th Earl of Angus

James, 4th Earl of Morton *m.* Elizabeth

Archibald, 8th Earl of Angus and
5th Earl of Morton (cousin)

Sir William Douglas of Lochleven,
6th Earl of Morton

Robert Douglas, Master of Morton

William Douglas, 7th Earl of Morton

The Buccleuch Family

Walter Scott. 1st Lord Scott of Buccleuch ('the bold Buccleuch')

Walter Scott, 1st Earl of Buccleuch

Francis Scott. 2nd Earl of Buccleuch *m.* **Margaret Leslie**

King Charles II

Mary, Countess of Buccleuch *m.* Walter Scott

Anna, 1st Duchess of Buccleuch *m.* James Scott,Duke of Monmouth

James,Scott, Earl of Dalkeith

Henry Scott, of Earl of Deloraine

James Douglas, 2nd Duke of Queensberry

Lady Jane Douglas *m.* **Francis Scott, 2nd Duke of Buccleuch**

George, Duke of Montagu

Francis Douglas Scott, Earl of Dalkeith *m.* **Caroline, daughter of Duke of Argyll**

Lady Elizabeth Montagu *m.* **Henry Douglas Scott, 3rd Duke of Buccleuch**

Charles Montagu Douglas Scott, 4th Duke of Buccleuch *m.* **Harriet Townshend**

Henry, Lord Montagu of Boughton

Walter Francis Montagu Douglas Scott, 5th Duke of Buccleuch

William, 6th Duke of Buccleuch

John, 7th Duke of Buccleuch

Walter, 8th Duke of Buccleuch

John, 9th Duke of Buccleuch

Richard, 10th Duke of Buccleuch

Appendix 2 Sources

Buccleuch papers, National Archives of Scotland

Buccleuch archives, Bowhill House

Aptel, Michael: Aberdour Castle (HMSO, 1996)

Balfour Paul, Sir J. (ed.): The Scots Peerage

Brigman, Nora: Dalkeith House (1989)

Brown, Iain Gordon: Rax me that Buik (Scala, 2010)

Brown, Michael: The Black Douglases (Tuckwell Press, 1998)

Buchan, John: Sir Walter Scott

Carrick, J.C.: Around Dalkeith and Camp Meg

'Country Life': articles on Dalkeith Palace (7 October 1911, 7 September 1935, 21 October 1993)

Duff, D. (ed.): Victoria in the Highlands, the personal journal of HM Queen Victoria

Dunbar, J.: The Historical Architecture of Scotland

Fraser, Sir William: Scotts of Buccleuch

Fraser, Sir William: Two Heiresses of Buccleuch

'Gardeners' Chronicle': article on Dalkeith Gardens, 20 January 1906

Giles, Jessica: History of Dalkeith House and Estate (Wisconsin Journal of Undergraduate Research, 2003)

Gloucester, HRH Princess Alice Duchess of: Memories of Ninety Years

Hibbert, Christopher: George IV, Regent and King 1811–1830

Hume, David of Godscroft: History of the House of Douglas and Angus (Mortimer and Macleod, Aberdeen, 1824)

Hunter, L.J.K.: Dalkeith House (special research essay, University of Edinburgh Architectural studies)

Lee, Maurice Jr: The Heiresses of Buccleuch

Macaulay, Dr James: The classical country house in Scotland, 1660–1800

Maxwell, Sir Herbert: History of the House of Douglas from the Earliest Times (Freemantle, 1902)

McIntosh, James: The Book of the Garden

Mudie: Historical Account of His Majesty's Visit to Scotland

'Pall Mall Magazine': article on Dalkeith Palace (Vol.16, September 1898)

Penman, Michael A.: David II, 1329–71

Prebble, John: The King's Jaunt (Birlinn, 1988)

Rae, John: Life of Adam Smith

Royal Commission for Ancient and Historical Monuments in Scotland: Inventory of Midlothian, volume 10 (and other documents)

Scott, Lord George Montagu Douglas: Fleeting Opportunities

Small, J.: The Castles and Mansions of the Lothians

Steuart, A Francis: Dalkeith, its Castle and Palace (Douglas and Foulis, Edinburgh 1925)

Stewart, John: The Grahams

Thomas, Jane – Midlothian: Illustrated Architectural Guide (Rutland Press, 1995)

Appendix 3 Photographic Credits

Scottish National Portrait Gallery

2.2 King James IV, 1473–1513, reigned 1488–1513 by unknown artist
2.3 King James VI, 1512–1542, father of Mary Queen of Scots, reigned 1513–1542 by unknown artist
3.1 James Douglas, 4th Earl of Morton, about 1516–1581, Regent of Scotland by Arnold Bronckhorst
4.1 King Charles I, 1600–1649, reigned 1625–1649 by the studio of Sir Anthony van Dyke
5.1 General George Monck, 1st Duke of Albemarle, 1608–1670, soldier and statesman by Sir Peter Lely and studio
5.2 Charles II, 1630–1685, King of Scots 1649–1685, King of England and Ireland, 1660–1685 by the studio of John Riley
7.2 Portrait of Prince Charles Edward Stuart, 1720–1788, eldest son of Prince James Francis Edward Stuart by Antonio David
7.4 Portrait of Adam Smith

The National Portrait Gallery

2.1 Margaret Tudor, 1489–1541, sister of Henry VIII.

Royal Commission on Ancient and Historical Monuments in Scotland

3.4 John Slezer's engraving of Dalkeith Palace
4.2 A 1639 map of Dalkeith Estate
7.6 The interior corridor of the Ice House
8.3 The Conservatory
8.4 The King's Gates
8.5 The arrival of Queen Victoria and Prince Albert at Dalkeith Palace
9.2 The Town Gates, decorated for the visit of King Edward VII
9.3 The Marble Hall, with the statue of the Duke of Wellington
9.4 The Dining Room
9.5 The Duchess's sitting room, with marble overmantel by Grinling Gibbons
9.6 The Library
9.7 The first-floor Gallery, where Queen Victoria held a Drawing Room
9.8 The Canaletto Room

National Archives of Scotland

1.2 The Arbroath Declaration

Museum of Scotland

3.3 Coin from Dalkeith Mint
3.5 The 'Maiden'

The Duke of Buccleuch

1.1 George Barret's painting of Dalkeith Palace from the River North Esk
3.2 Mary, Queen of Scots (the Dalkeith portrait)
5.3 The Duke of Monmouth
5.4 Kneller's portrait of Anna, Duchess of Buccleuch and her sons
6.1 Ground floor plan of Dalkeith Palace
6.2 The Palace as it was designed by James Smith
6.4 Smeaton House, later known as East Park
7.1 The Stable Block
7.3 Henry, 3rd Duke of Buccleuch
7.5 Duke Henry with his family; Montagu Bridge in background
7.7 Robert Adam's design for the Montagu Bridge
7.8 The Montagu Bridge as it is now
7.9 Charles, 4th Duke of Buccleuch
7.10 Raeburn's portrait of Sir Walter Scott
8.1 Sir David Wilkie's portrait of King George IV
8.2 Walter Francis, 5th Duke of Buccleuch
9.1 William, 6th Duke of Buccleuch
10.1 The plan for the new Visitor Centre and Cafe

Index

Index

Names in the order in which they appear in the text

De Graham of Dalkeith, Sir William 17
David I, King 17, 21
Henry I of England, King 17
De Graham of Abercorn and Dalkeith, Sir Peter 17, 24
De Graham, Sir Henry 19
William I, King (William the Lion) 19
Alexander II, King 19
Alexander III, King 19
Margaret, Queen (the 'Maid of Norway') 20
De Graham, Sir Nicholas 20, 21
Edward I of England, King 20
Balliol, John, King 22
Bruce, Robert, Lord of Annandale 21, 23n
Bruce, Robert, Earl of Carrick 22, 23n
Bruce, Robert (King Robert I) 22, 23n
Wallace, William 22
Graham, Sir John 22
Edward II of England, King 23, 23n
Edward III of England, King 23, 24, 27
Douglas, Sir William 24, 27, 28
Douglas, Archibald, Lord of 29n
Aberdour Castle 50
Hermitage Castle 28, 29, 31
David II, King 28, 30
Ramsay, Sir Alexander of Dalhousie 27, 28
Douglas, William, 1st Earl of 29
Douglas, Sir James, Lord of Dalkeith 30, 31, 34
Douglas, Archibald (Archibald the Grim) 30, 31, 32, 34
Robert II, King 33n
St Nicholas Church, Dalkeith 32, 35, 71n
Angus, 1st Earl of 32
Douglas, Sir James, 1st Lord Dalkeith 33
Douglas, James, 2nd Lord Dalkeith 33
Gifford, James, of Sheriffhall 33
Douglas, Henry, of Borgue 33
James II, King 33n, 34
Douglas, James, 1st Earl of Morton 34
Douglas, William, 8th Earl of 33–34
James IV, King 34, 35, 37
Douglas, John, 2nd Earl of Morton 35–36
Tudor, Margaret, Queen 35, 38n, 45n
Holyroodhouse, Palace of 11, 36, 104, 125, 138
Douglas, James, 3rd Earl of 37
James V, King 38
Angus, 7th Earl of 41
Douglas, Robert, of Lochleven, 6th Earl of Morton 38
Mary, Queen of Scots 38n, 149
Douglas, Sir George, of Pittendreich 38
Douglas, James, 4th Earl of Morton 41–53
Henry VIII of England, King 35, 38n, 41
Beaton, Cardinal 41
Arran, Earl of, Regent of Scotland 41
Angus, 8th Earl of and 5th Earl of Morton 41, 44
Mary of Guise, Queen 44, 45
Darnley, Lord 45, 52
Lennox, Countess of 45, 45n
Rizzio, David 45
Bothwell, 1st Earl of 46–47
James VI of Scotland and I of England, King 59, 67
Stewart, Esme, Duke of Lennox 53, 57
Stewart, Captain James 53
Maxwell, John, 8th Lord 57
Douglas, William, 7th Earl of Morton 59–63
Charles I, King 12, 50n, 60, 61n, 161
Traquair, Earl of 61, 93
Leslie, General Alexander, 1st Earl of Leven 61, 69
Scott, Francis, 2nd Earl of Buccleuch 63
Scott, Walter, Lord Scott of Buccleuch 67
Armstrong, William of Kinmont 67n
Scott, Walter, 1st Earl of Buccleuch 67

Leslie, Margaret, Countess of Buccleuch 69
Bothwell, 5th Earl of 67
Scott, Mary, Countess of Buccleuch 70, 73–74, 78
Scott, Anna, 1st Duchess of Buccleuch 12, 69
Cromwell, Oliver 12, 70
Monck, General George, 1st Duke of Albemarle 12, 70, 71n
Wemyss, Earl of 73
Tweeddale, Earl of 73
Scott, Sir Gideon of Highchester 73
Charles II, King 70, 125
Cromwell, Richard 75
Melville, George, Lord 78
Rothes, Earl of 69, 70, 78
Crofts, James, later James Scott, 1st Duke of Monmouth and Buccleuch 79–84
Pepys, Samuel 79
James, Duke of York, later King James II 80, 83–84
Mary II, Queen 85
Kneller, Sir Godfrey 82
Scott, James, Earl of Dalkeith 97
Scott, Henry, Earl of Deloraine 82, 99
Cornwallis, Lord 84, 85
William III, King 85n, 89, 97
Smith, James 12, 89, 94
Drumlanrig Castle, Dumfriesshire 43n, 89, 112, 159n
Anne, Queen 82, 97, 99, 151
George I, King 97
Royston, James Mackenzie, Lord 97
Adam, William 11, 98, 104
Defoe, Daniel 99
Scott, Francis, 2nd Duke of Buccleuch 97
East Park (Smeaton House) 98, 103, 104, 113, 150
Charles Edward Stuart, Prince 104
Scott, Francis, Earl of Dalkeith 106
Caroline Park, Granton 136
Bowhill, Selkirkshire 106, 112, 113, 120, 126, 129, 131, 133, 140, 147, 153, 157, 158
Scott, Henry, 3rd Duke of Buccleuch 107–117
Smith, Adam 108, 109, 110, 111
Monthermer, Marquis of 109, 111
Montagu, 3rd Duke of 111
Boughton House, Northamptonshire 111, 131, 149
Queensberry, 4th Duke of ('Old Q') 111, 135
Scott, Charles Montagu Douglas, 4th Duke of Buccleuch 112, 118–122
Scott, Henry Montagu Douglas, Lord Montagu of Boughton 112, 125, 128, 129, 131
Adam, Robert 11, 114, 114n
Queensberry, 3rd Duke of 114
Dundas, Henry, Viscount Melville 116
Scott, Sir Walter 113n, 118, 120, 120n, 125
Scott, Walter Francis Montagu Douglas, 5th Duke of Buccleuch 124, 135
George IV, King 11, 12, 94, 125, 132, 135n, 136, 137, 148, 153, 160, 161
Burn, William 132, 135
St Mary's Church, Dalkeith Park 140, 153, 159
Montagu House, London 135, 135n, 145, 147, 157, 158
Victoria, Queen 12, 94, 136, 137, 139, 139n, 147
Scott, William Montagu Douglas, 6th Duke of Buccleuch 145–147
Gladstone, William Ewart 145
Langholm Lodge, Dumfriessshire 147, 158
Edward VII, King 12, 147
George V, King 12, 148, 153
Scott, John Montagu Douglas, 7th Duke of Buccleuch 157
Gloucester, Princess Alice, Duchess of 157, 157n
Scott, Walter Montagu Douglas, 8th Duke of Buccleuch 159
International Computers Limited 159
Scott John Montagu Douglas, 9th Duke of Buccleuch 160
Wisconsin, University of 12, 13, 160
Scott, Richard Montagu Douglas, 10th Duke of Buccleuch 160

45221953R00105

Printed in Poland
by Amazon Fulfillment
Poland Sp. z o.o., Wrocław